SO-EID-433

Suzanne Allman is an American woman

In her teens Suzanne was starry-eyed and went to New York with an aspiring musician. Shortly thereafter the musician ran off to search for his Muse. In her twenties Suzanne was practical, working long hours to support herself and her daughter. Now she's in her late thirties and a new age is dawning: the age of revolt.

Her college-bound daughter is leaving the nest and Suzanne is leaving Manhattan. She's got money in her pocket, an itch to see America and a feeling that life has something wonderful in store for her. Anything might happen, and when it happens, Suzanne will welcome it with open arms.

Dear Reader,

This is indeed a special year for American Romance: it marks our fifth anniversary of bringing you the love stories you want to read. Stories of real women of contemporary America—women just like you. This month we're celebrating that anniversary with a special four-book series by four of your favorite American Romance authors. Rebecca Flanders, Beverly Sommers, Judith Arnold and Anne Stuart introduce you to Jaime, Suzanne, Abbie and Marielle—the women of Yorktown Towers.

They've been neighbors, they've been friends, but now they're saying goodbye, leaving Manhattan one by one, in search of their lives, in search of happiness, carving out their own version of the American Dream.

Jaime, Suzanne, Abbie and Marielle: four believable American Romance heroines... four contemporary American women just like you.

We hope you enjoy these special stories as much as we enjoyed preparing them for you for this occasion. It's our way of saying thanks for being there these past five years. We here at American Romance look forward to many more anniversaries of success....

Debra Matteucci
Senior Editor

Reach for the Sky
Beverly Sommers

Harlequin Books

TORONTO • NEW YORK • LONDON
AMSTERDAM • PARIS • SYDNEY • HAMBURG
STOCKHOLM • ATHENS • TOKYO • MILAN

Published August 1988

First printing June 1988

ISBN 0-373-16258-8

Chapter One

"Where are we, anyway, Mom?"

"Ohio."

"You sure? How can you tell?"

"I can read the signs. We're now in the Midwest, I believe. If you want to know exactly where we are, Mouse, you could get out the road map." Not that she would; neither of them liked to read maps.

"It doesn't look any different than Pennsylvania," said Mouse.

"Don't complain to me, I didn't make the country."

"We're in a good mood today, aren't we?"

"Actually, I'm in a very good mood," said Suzanne, "considering the hour. It's gorgeous out, isn't it?"

"Right now, but wait until later."

"Well, let's enjoy it while it's still cool and worry about the heat when it arrives."

At least by the time it heated up they'd both be in good moods. Neither of them was at her best in the morning and only the fact that Suzanne liked to have them settled in a motel room before dark got them started on the road at a fairly early hour of the day.

"I don't know about you, Mom, but I'm getting pretty tired of all the trees. You'd think they'd cut some of them down and put up buildings."

Suzanne was also getting tired of all the trees. She was used to seeing trees in parks, not scattered all over the place, and here not even scattered but dense. "I think we've lived in New York too long."

"Too long? I've lived there all my life."

"Well, I'm afraid we're going to have trees for scenery the entire trip. And farmland. We ought to run into some farms along the way."

"No desert?"

"Didn't they teach you geography at Dalton?"

"Sure, which is how I know there's a desert somewhere in this country. I think it's near the Grand Canyon, Mom."

"We're not going that far west. Colorado's in the Rocky Mountains and the desert is on the other side."

"Probably just as well," said Mouse. "With the air conditioner we have, we'd probably die in the desert."

Suzanne was beginning to think she should have gone for comfort rather than style. She could have bought a car with a good air conditioner and a tape deck to keep Mouse happy and tinted windows to keep the sun out and enough legroom to stretch out. There wasn't even a back seat to curl up in if one of them wanted a nap, just two little seats that looked more like jump seats than anything else. But she had taken one look at this car and fallen in love with its looks, which was never a good reason to fall in love.

"How about cities?" asked Mouse. "Do we go through any cities?"

"I was hoping to avoid them, but if you really feel the need of a city, we can always stop in Chicago."

"Is it as big as New York?"

"No."

"Does it have a Bloomingdale's?"

"I don't think so."

"Well, what does it have?"

"A lake," said Suzanne. "I believe it has a lake."

"Big deal," said Mouse. "Central Park has a lake."

Suzanne was a little sorry she had taken a long detour to show Mouse Niagara Falls. Now it would probably be the Rocky Mountains before she could impress her again to anywhere near that extent, and they had a lot of more mundane scenery to cover in between.

Suzanne might be getting tired of the trees, but she was still impressed with the sky. It was a novelty to be able to see the sky—and so much of it—without having to lean back her head and stare straight up.

What she'd like to do is get off the tree-lined highway and see where the people lived. She'd like to see some houses and schools and shopping centers, some indication that there were people in the world besides the ones in the cars and the service areas. She had the idea that if you stayed on the interstates long enough your vision of the country would become one of people constantly on the go, never settling down. Sometimes it seemed that the whole world was trying to pass her on the highway. Trying and succeeding because the Suzuki wasn't fast enough to pass anything, not even the mobile homes being towed or the campers.

That's what she'd do later after she dropped Mouse off at college. She would take all the time she wanted to go everywhere, seeing how other people lived, while she tried to decide where she wanted to live.

Not Ohio, though. Ohio was no doubt very nice, but Suzanne longed for open spaces and sky that reached from horizon to horizon. She wanted a place where the sense of the place spoke of the same freedom she was feeling at the prospect of Mouse leaving home for the first time. She would know the place when she saw it. She'd know it because it would fit.

Freedom was the magic word. All she had to do was say "freedom" out loud or even think "freedom" and the most wonderful sense of expectation filled her. Freedom was being able to live wherever she wanted. Freedom was being able to quit a job she hated and having enough money saved not to have to worry about the next job for a very long time. Maybe never. Freedom was having Mouse going off to college, the first step in going off on her own in the world. She was going to have the rest of her life to do exactly what she wanted.

Suzanne spotted the sign at the side of the highway. It announced the third lookout point they had come to that day, and the morning was only half over. Suzanne desperately wanted a cigarette and since Mouse, in the two days they had been on the road, had said, "Oh, look, let's stop here," at least twice an hour and sometimes more every time Suzanne was at the wheel, this time Suzanne decided to pull the same thing on Mouse. She could smoke and Mouse could look to her heart's content and both of them would be happy. Freedom would be being able to smoke whenever she wanted without Mouse giving her a lecture on her health.

When Suzanne was at the wheel she enjoyed driving so much after so many years of rarely getting an opportunity to drive that she hardly ever wanted to stop. Sitting in the passenger seat while Mouse practiced her driving, however, was slightly hard on her nerves. When she was driving she wished she had something faster. When Mouse drove, the Suzuki four-wheel drive seemed to her to speed down the road like a Formula I car. Mouse had only started taking driving lessons that summer and had gotten her license because the man seemed to take pity on her rather than because of any driving skill.

And having to shift wasn't making things any easier for Mouse. The car she had been taught on had an automatic transmission, and Mouse had as yet to master the shifting on the Suzuki. Suzanne had bought the Suzuki because it was very cute to look at and economical to drive, but it was slow and she was also getting tired of shifting and it couldn't be called the most comfortable car in the world. They had only been on the road a short time that morning and already Suzanne was uncomfortable from being bounced around so much.

"Why don't you pull in up ahead and we'll take a look?" Suzanne suggested, trying to sound as though she were only casually interested.

"Here?" asked Mouse, sounding surprised that her mother was the one suggesting a stop.

"I thought you liked lookout points," said Suzanne, grabbing her handbag from behind the seat and digging her hand down in its depths to locate her cigarettes and lighter. "Anyway, I feel like stretching; I'm getting stiff."

"You just want to smoke," groused Mouse.

"That's right."

"You smoked three at breakfast."

"Don't start on me this early," said Suzanne, who was always amazed Mouse could count to three. The progressive schools she had gone to had been more interested in forming the creative child than teaching such ordinary things as arithmetic and spelling.

Suzanne was feeling a sense of exhilaration that she was up so early, that the day was still cool, and that while she might feel the slightest of urges to smack Mouse for counting her cigarettes, all in all they were getting along pretty well considering they were in each other's face twenty-four hours of every day, and Mouse wasn't able to go into her room, slam the door and call up her friends every time she got irritated. "Anyway, I knew it would be my last chance for a while. If you let me smoke in the car, I wouldn't smoke so many at meals."

"All this fresh air, it's a shame to pollute it."

"You've become an environmentalist now?"

"All right, if you insist," said Mouse in the tone of a martyr, a tone she had damn near perfected and that made her sound so much like Barbara Jean was required to sound in *Reach for the Sky* that it was all Suzanne could do not to laugh when she used it.

Mouse pulled off the highway a little too fast and Suzanne, who was having trouble finding her lighter amidst all the stuff in her handbag, didn't look up, merely said, "Slow down a little," and then Mouse said, "Hey, look at the cowboy," and Suzanne, wondering what a cowboy was doing in Ohio, looked up in time to see Mouse, her face turned away from the windshield for a moment, momentarily lose control of the car and sideswipe a large black sedan that was pulled up to the guardrail. And that was all she saw of the cowboy for the moment because something very nightmarish happened then, and while it seemed to happen in slow motion, it happened too fast for her to do anything about it.

It started as just a sound, the sound of metal crunching against metal, and then there was movement where there shouldn't have been movement, and then Suzanne was yelling, "Stop the car!" and reaching over and pulling up the emergency brake herself, while her other hand was fumbling with the handle on the car door.

She leaped out of the car in time to hear a second sound, that of splintering wood, and it didn't take a genius to figure out what was making that sound. The large black sedan was slowly going through the guardrail. Suzanne ran for the car as though to stop its momentum all by herself, and got there in time to see the sedan roll almost all the way through the guardrail, which had appeared to snap in two.

And then, as Suzanne watched, the black sedan tilted, slowly, very slowly, before falling over the side of the cliff. It looked like a shiny metal toy as it tumbled end over end, the black metal vivid against the green foliage. For a moment it came to rest at the bottom, looking like a broken toy, and she was thinking it was going to be hard to get it back up the side of the cliff, but almost as soon as she thought that, there was an explosion and she watched in shock as the car went up in flames.

"Oh, shit, Mom; Mom, what're we gonna do? I knocked that car over, maybe I killed someone. There might've been a baby in that car, Mom, or a dog."

Mouse's mounting hysteria got through Suzanne's shock and she put her arms around the girl to try to calm her. But Mouse was shaking all over and sobbing now, and Suzanne pulled her back from the edge, not wanting her daughter to slip and follow the car over the cliff.

"Did you see anyone in that car, Mom? Did you see anyone?"

"I couldn't tell," said Suzanne. "The windows were tinted. But I don't think so. I think they would have had time to get out, or at least we would have heard screams."

"Then who does the car belong to?"

Suzanne heard a noise behind her, the sound of something scraping gravel. The cowboy, she thought, belatedly remembering the reason her daughter's eyes had been momentarily diverted from the road.

She turned around and there he was, slowly making his way over to them on crutches. She saw him stumble and reach out a hand to steady himself on the back of their Suzuki. He was indeed a cowboy, with the requisite boots and skinny jeans and worn cowboy hat. He also had a leg brace on his left leg and wooden crutches propped underneath his arms. But while his leg might look bad, his face looked worse. He looked as shocked as she was feeling. All the blood seemed to have drained from his face as he stared at the space where the car had been. And it must have been his car unless he came by horse, and that seemed doubtful.

"Was there anyone in the car?" she asked him.

He shook his head.

"Thank God," said Suzanne, and felt her daughter's sobs subside somewhat.

Mouse wiped her eyes with the back of her hand and pulled out of Suzanne's arms. "Was there anything alive in there? A pet or anything?" she asked the cowboy.

He seemed finally able to speak. "Nope. Just my gear."

"I'm so sorry," said Mouse, "it was all my fault. If I hadn't seen you and looked away for a second...I've only been driving for about a month."

"Be quiet, Mouse," warned Suzanne.

"What?"

"I said be quiet. You barely touched that car. If he'd had it in park it wouldn't have gone over that easily."

The slightest glimmer of awareness could be detected in the cowboy's eyes beneath the shaded brim of his hat. "Are you anticipating a lawsuit, ma'am?" he asked in a slow cadence.

Suzanne, being a New Yorker, always anticipated lawsuits. "Was it in park?" she asked him.

"Mom, what difference does it make? I knocked it over. It wasn't his fault, he wasn't anywhere near it."

"Please be quiet, Mouse. Go look at the view."

Mouse turned astonished eyes in her direction. "Look at the *view*? I just *ruined* the view!"

One side of the cowboy's mouth was starting to turn up. "I wouldn't worry about it, ma'am; I'm sure your insurance covers it." He looked at Mouse. "And don't you be worrying yourself about my car. It was only a rental and had no sentimental value for me whatsoever. Now my pharmacy in there, that's something to worry about. If I don't get a pain pill soon, I might collapse over the side of that cliff myself. You wouldn't happen to have something strong for pain on you, would you? Even an aspirin would be appreciated."

Mouse looked at her mother. Suzanne shook her head. "I have tranquilizers, though, and I'm sure we all could use one."

"*Mom,*" said Mouse, who didn't approve of tranquilizers.

"Thank you, ma'am, but I don't feel the need to be tranquil, I'd just like my knee to stop hurting. But I appreciate the offer."

Suzanne reached for her cigarettes, got one lit, then looked down the side of the cliff again, hoping against hope that what she had seen really hadn't happened and that the cowboy's car, all in one piece, would be sitting there waiting to be retrieved. It was sitting there, all right, but it no longer bore much resemblance to a car. Smoke was pouring out of the wreckage.

"You mustn't have had the brake on," Suzanne said, "or it wouldn't have just rolled like that. I'll bet you didn't put your emergency brake on."

The cowboy took her measure in a long look. "It was fine until it got shoved by that red toy of yours," he observed.

"Mom, quit giving him a hard time," said Mouse, coming to the cowboy's defense. "His car would still be sitting there, perfectly safe, if I hadn't run into it."

Suzanne knew she was in the wrong but couldn't seem to help herself. It was a lack of trust in mankind in general and men in particular. It was paranoia of a type that New Yorkers breathed in like air. It was the kind of thing that made a normally calm person pop a tranquilizer on occasion. It was a condition she was hoping to get rid of once she was free of New York, but it hadn't happened yet.

"Just look at him," Mouse persisted. "The poor guy's standing there in pain—a cripple." She turned to the cowboy. "What happened, did you break your leg?"

"No, it's not a broken leg," he said.

"Well, anyway, he's in bad shape, Mom, and all you're worried about is getting sued."

"No," said Suzanne, "I'm not worried about getting sued; I'm worried about you. I'm worried about what they do to teenage drivers in Ohio who recklessly endanger lives."

That shut Mouse up and made the cowboy chuckle.

He was just starting to say something when he broke off and they could all hear the sound of a siren in the distance.

"I believe help's on the way," the cowboy said.

They stood silently as the siren got closer and closer, finally watching as a state police car pulled off the road and stopped behind them. There was no movement in the car for a moment, and then both doors opened and two troopers stepped out of the car.

With a nod in their direction, the troopers walked over to the broken guardrail and looked down. Suzanne hoped they'd be more helpful than they looked. Neither of them looked any older than Mouse. One was a blonde with his hat set rakishly back on his head and mirror sunglasses, and the other was a redhead with freckled skin so smooth Suzanne would swear he didn't shave yet. They both looked like little boys dressed up in costumes. The cowboy on crutches inspired more confidence than these two.

"Anyone see it go over?" the redhead asked.

"We all saw it," said Mouse.

"How many in the car?" the blonde asked, sounding somewhat nervous, as though he were going to be required to pull dead bodies out of the wreckage.

"It was my car," said the cowboy. "No one was in it."

The trooper seemed to lighten up. "Glad to hear that," the blonde said. "Who does the Suzuki belong to?"

"It belongs to me," said Suzanne.

"Well, folks," said the redhead, "would someone like to tell us what happened here?"

"It was an accident," said Suzanne, wanting to make that clear from the start. "Our car just happened to brush against his car when we pulled in here, and for no discernible reason, his car ended up down there."

There was a brief period of silence as the troopers no doubt wondered at the simplicity of her explanation. Suzanne figured the less said the better.

"What kind of car were you driving, sir?" the blond trooper asked the cowboy.

"An Oldsmobile."

The trooper was nodding. "Right. And a tiny little Suzuki just happened to brush against that quite substantial Olds of yours and your Olds went flying off the cliff?"

There seemed to be a muscle jumping at the corner of the cowboy's mouth. "I wouldn't exactly describe it as flying; it was more like a slow roll."

The redhead said to Suzanne, "I'd like to see your driver's license, ma'am."

Suzanne reached into her handbag and located her wallet. She handed over her driver's license, then lit up another cigarette.

The trooper slowly read it, then handed it to his partner. "New York City, right, ma'am?" He sounded as though he had solved a puzzle.

"That's right," said Suzanne, instantly on the defensive. She'd put down New York all she wanted, but she wouldn't stand by while other people did.

The blond trooper was grinning. "New Yorkers. They'll do it to you every time."

The redhead was nodding. "The thing about New Yorkers is, all year long they take taxicabs and subways and buses, and then along comes summer and they decide to go for a little drive, only New Yorkers don't know how to drive and they end up being a danger to everyone else on the road."

"You don't look like you're from New York," said the blonde, looking over at the cowboy.

"Wyoming," said the cowboy.

"Right," said the blonde. "Did you put your car in park when you got out of it?"

"I don't remember, but judging by the ease with which it went over the cliff, I'd have to say I probably didn't."

The redhead grinned. "Of course horses don't have park."

Almost unconsciously, Suzanne and Mouse and the cowboy were drawing closer, as though to form a block against the two troopers.

The blonde said, "What do you think, Chris, do we run them in?"

"Oh, we run them in all right, Daryl. This isn't just writing out a ticket. This is the kind of an accident that could take hours to sort out."

"There's nothing to sort out," said Mouse. "I was driving and I was at fault and you can take my driver's license away if you want, but my mom and the cowboy are innocent."

Mouse could have been speaking to herself for all the notice the troopers took of her. "I'm afraid you're going to have to come in town with us, ma'am, and go through a few formalities," Suzanne was told.

"It's going to be some small town where they lock us up and no one ever hears from us again," said Mouse, her overly imaginative mind going to work.

"This is Ohio," said the blonde, who was now giving Mouse the eye, "and no one disappears."

"This is rural America and you probably make all your money by giving tickets to tourists," countered Mouse.

"Be quiet, Mouse," warned Suzanne.

"Oh, let her keep talking, ma'am," said the blonde trooper. "It's just such a treat to hear a New Yorker shoot off her mouth. Why, we just wait all year for the summer to come so that we get to meet some of you sophisticated, witty big-city folk in person." He turned to the cowboy, a big grin splitting his face, and said, "Don't you agree, Wyoming? I'll bet you just can't wait for these two to come rolling into your state. Just watch it that they don't come anywhere near the horse you're riding.''

Suzanne could see Mouse starting to burn. Having been brought up in New York, she could be as assertive and bigmouthed as the best of them, and when she opened her mouth, Suzanne wasn't surprised at what came out.

Mouse took a step toward the troopers and crossed her arms. ''Why, you little punk,'' said Mouse to the blonde, although the trooper was a good foot taller than her. ''I'll bet you've never set foot out of your hick town your entire life. Makes you feel like a big man wearing that uniform, doesn't it? Makes you feel real good to bully two females and a cripple, I'll bet. Why, you wouldn't dare set foot in New York because the city would eat you up and spit you out!''

Instead of taking offense, as Suzanne anticipated, the blonde looked her daughter up and down and then started to laugh. Before he could launch into a counterattack, Suzanne said, ''Please, could we just take care of whatever needs taking care of? We have a man in pain here who should probably be off his leg.''

''Don't worry about me, ma'am,'' said the cowboy. ''I was enjoying it.''

The blond trooper pulled his eyes away from Mouse and said to the cowboy, ''Do you think you'd be able to manage a clutch?''

''I could try,'' said the cowboy.

''We'd appreciate it if you could follow us into town in their car.''

''Seeing as we're such dangerous suspects, you don't want to let us out of your sight,'' said Mouse.

The trooper grinned. ''I'm more worried about the other cars on the road,'' he told her.

"I don't think he should be driving with that leg," said Suzanne.

The cowboy held up his hands in surrender. "Whoa. I'm perfectly capable of driving your car, ma'am, and I promise you I'll get it there in one piece. Where I come from, if a man can't handle a four-wheel drive, he's not a man."

"Save me from macho cowboys," murmured Suzanne to Mouse as they got into the back seat of the police car.

"I think he was just being funny," said Mouse. "Anyway, I thought you liked cowboys."

"Oh, I do," agreed Suzanne. "But the liberated side of me just had to say that." And she did like cowboys, always had, but the only ones she had ever really seen had been larger than life on the movie screen. Maybe they weren't all they appeared to be in movies. Maybe they were just regular men, like any she had ever met, dressed up in cowboy clothes.

As they started up, Suzanne asked, "Am I allowed to smoke in here?"

"Afraid not, ma'am," said the blonde in the passenger seat.

Suzanne turned in time to see the smirk on Mouse's face. "Mouse, I know I smoked nonstop back there, but it was a crisis. You obviously don't understand the meaning of addiction."

"I never saw anyone more calm," said Mouse. "You just saw your opportunity to sneak a few more smokes, that's all."

"I wasn't calm, believe me."

Mouse snorted. "I'm getting hysterical and you're calmly looking over the edge of the cliff as though you see cars being totaled every day."

"Trying to give it up?" asked the blonde, turning around in his seat to look at Suzanne.

"Yes," she said.

"I gave up smoking three years ago," he told her, which failed to impress Suzanne as she could have given up smoking at that age, too. He then turned his full attention to Mouse. "Did she call you Mouse?" he asked her, his mouth already forming into a smile.

Suzanne watched the metamorphosis of teenager into adult woman as Mouse shifted around in the seat and did everything but bat her eyelashes at the trooper. "It's actually Melissa," she said.

The trooper's smile turned into a sexy grin. "I'm Daryl, and that's Chris, driving."

Suzanne could see Chris's eyes on Mouse in the rearview mirror and she felt like telling him to keep them on the road.

"So what's happening?" asked Mouse. "We being arrested or something?"

"Is that the way they do things in New York?" asked Daryl

"We're pretty civilized in New York," said Mouse.

Daryl and Chris both laughed. "That's not what we hear," said Daryl.

"If you want to live a civilized existence, it's the only place to be."

"Where you folks headed?" Daryl asked Mouse.

"Colorado. I'm going to college there."

"If New York's all that great, why're you going to Colorado to college?"

That silenced Mouse for a moment, and into the silence Suzanne said, "She likes to ski."

"Mom, I told you that wasn't the only reason I'm going there."

"I know what you told me, but I didn't believe you."

"We don't have any skiing in Ohio," said Chris.

"All I've seen so far are a lot of trees," said Mouse.

Daryl was carefully scrutinizing Mouse, from her jeans with the knees torn out to her skimpy tank top.

"You sure could use some new jeans," observed Daryl. "You look like you went over the cliff with that car."

Mouse looked at her mother and rolled her eyes. The jeans had cost eighty-five dollars simply because they had been made to look old and worn and it was only the second time Mouse had worn them.

Suzanne had laughed when she'd seen them. She could remember when buying used jeans in the sixties had been the big thing, when everyone was trying to look like a hippie. Now the fashion was back again, but this time they weren't used jeans, they were designer specials.

By the time they reached the town, Mouse and the boys had exchanged life stories, which hadn't taken up much time as none of them had lived that long. By then, Suzanne had visions of their trip across the country not being the educational experience she had anticipated, but a series of teenage flirtations. Mouse was all but hanging over the seat talking to Daryl, and Suzanne was wishing she had opted to drive the Suzuki and let the cowboy in for all this scintillating talk.

Suzanne turned and looked out the back window and saw their red Suzuki following them. The poor guy. He lost his car, he lost any luggage he might have had with him, he was in pain, and there he was driving a car that had very little in the way of shocks and was probably doing damage to his knee. And he hadn't complained once. A New Yorker would have taken three of her Valiums and had a nervous breakdown, anyway.

Living in Wyoming must be good on the nerves.

Chapter Two

The town looked as though it might have once been quaint but was now merely depressed. Billy pulled into the space behind the police car and watched as the girl and her mother and the two troopers went into the small wooden building with the state police crest on the door. His knee was aching, his left leg was having muscle spasms, and he wondered what latent bit of machismo residing in him had been responsible for his not only insisting to his doctor and his family that he could drive all the way from New York to Wyoming, but also for telling the troopers that he could drive a car with a clutch. He could drive all day in the Olds with his leg not hurting him as much as a few minutes in the Suzuki.

It had been more than just a fear of flying that had possessed him to drive to Wyoming, though, because, after all, he had flown to New York, even though any choice had really been out of his hands and he had been sedated enough so that he had barely noticed he was flying. He could have flown back, too, in the sure knowledge that he had enough painkillers with him to effectively dull the pain as well as any lurking fear he always got with someone else in control of his destiny. It had been, he reckoned, a direct result of having to use crutches, of having to rely on something besides his own two legs to get him around, that had made him stubbornly resist all dissuasion and rent a car. If he couldn't walk properly, damn it, then he could sure as hell drive. Because if he couldn't walk *and* couldn't drive, then he was a sorry excuse for a man.

Or so he had told himself. Especially in a car that had no clutch so that his left leg could stretch out, immobile, and his good leg could do all the work.

Except he thought maybe that was the problem: the immobility. He was supposed to be doing exercises every day to bend the knee, not leave it in one position during hours of driving. He'd only been driving a couple of hours today and his leg was already stiff by the time he stopped at that lookout. And that had been the only reason he had stopped. It certainly hadn't been because he thought some lookout in Ohio was worth looking at. They thought that was scenery? They ought to see Wyoming. That little cliff wouldn't have even counted for a hill in Wyoming.

And then because of his macho stance, because of his leg spasms when he got out of the car, he had been as much responsible for his car going off the cliff as the girl. He really didn't have any recollection of putting the car in park. As close as he could recall, he had stopped the car and opened the door and swung his bad leg out, followed by his good one, and then he had taken the first tentative steps in order to flex his knee and try to work some of the stiffness out. The last thing on his mind had been the danger of his car suddenly rolling over the cliff by itself. Which it wouldn't have done, really, although if that car of theirs could nudge it over so easily then perhaps something as simple as his leaning against it might have done the very same thing. He hadn't leaned against it, though. He had retrieved his crutches from the back seat and set off at a slow pace, and looking at the scenery hadn't even entered into it. Just flexing his knee in a spot where there were no other people to watch him had been his agenda.

Other people not watching him had been one of his priorities. Everyone had some story when they saw his leg brace and crutches. Everyone had had a knee injury at some time and wanted to compare notes. Most of the ones he had heard about so far had to do with sports; several from running; a couple from tennis; and one from football. He didn't want to hear those stories. He particularly didn't like the point at which the story had been told and then it was his turn to describe how he injured his knee and he had to admit to having a horse fall on him. When you're wearing boots and a Stetson, which pretty much advertised to the world that you spent some time on horses, about the last thing you wanted to admit was that something as stupid as a horse falling on you actually happened.

Yes, the girl should have watched where she was going and not nudged his car that way, and yes, her insurance company would probably have several fits when they heard about it but end up paying anyway, but the fact of the matter was, if he had put the car in park there was very little reason to suppose it would have gone over. Not without a real concerted effort by another car or a couple of people setting out to manually shove it over.

It wasn't just the car that went over. There was the leather bag he was rather fond of, the one that was just worn enough to look well used without being so worn it looked worn out, and inside that bag, along with a couple of changes of clothes and his shaving gear, were the bandages and painkillers and sleeping pills and the rest of the paraphernalia his doctor had thought he might need for the trip. And in the back seat had been the walker, which he didn't mind seeing go over because he'd be damned if he was going to ever use that walker again, and his Levi jacket in case it got cold, and the thing that looked like a giant rubber band to exercise his foot with and assorted books he had taken to the hospital, not knowing he'd be sharing his room with a nonstop television viewer who never turned the set off long enough for Billy to even open a book.

And, in the glove compartment, had been his wallet. He was now without money and the credit card he used for gas and any means of identification whatsoever. He didn't even have a driver's license. He shouldn't have even driven the Suzuki, although, since it was at the suggestion of the trooper, he didn't see how not having a license could get him in trouble. He didn't even have to say he was Billy Blue. He could introduce himself as anyone and there'd be no way to dispute his claim. Except for the car-rental agency. That kind of thing wouldn't wash with them. And weren't they going to be thrilled to hear that nice new Olds was now at the bottom of some gulch with about enough left of it to stick in some trash bag and tote away.

So what should he do next? Should he call his sister collect and have her wire him some money and then get to Cleveland and catch the next plane out of there home? Should he insist that the car-rental agency immediately replace his car and continue the trip even though he was pretty sure that at the rate he was going, which was something slightly faster than a snail's pace considering a couple of hundred miles of driving left him exhausted, it might be next spring before he reached Wyoming? Should he turn around and go back to New York and

admit to his doctor that he was wrong and the doctor was
right and he wanted to crawl back into that hospital bed
and hide out and be taken care of until his leg was back
to normal? If it ever was going to be back to normal.

Or should he—and this was a possibility that had been
floating around the back of his mind ever since he got his
first good look at her—throw himself upon the mercy of
that sweet-looking New York woman, playing upon her
guilt, playing upon her sympathy, playing upon anything he could come up with, and beg her to drive him
home?

The only problem with that scenario was that they
might be headed back to New York for all he knew. Or
Cleveland might be their destination, in which case they
were almost there. He had mentioned Wyoming and neither of them had spoken up and said, "Oh, we're on our
way to Wyoming." No one had said anything like that,
and driving him home might be a couple of thousand
miles out of their way. And they might be feeling guilty,
but surely there were limits to guilt.

He thought he just might give it a try, though. But it
was more for ulterior motives than because he actually
fancied traveling more than a mile in the back seat of this
uncomfortable little excuse for a four-wheel drive. And
the ulterior motive at work had more to do with the
woman than with her daughter's poor driving.

There was the little matter of the woman's looks. The
fact that if one of his nurses or if one of the other patients had looked like this woman looked, maybe he
wouldn't have been in such an all-fired hurry to be dis-
charged. He might seem like a dumb Westerner to sharp,
fast-talking New Yorkers, but he wasn't so dumb he
would have complained about the hospital if there had
been someone with *her* looks taking care of him.

He'd been trying to figure out her age, but that had been impossible. If he had seen her alone he would figure her for his age, maybe a little younger, although Wendy was his age and Wendy already had lines that this woman probably wouldn't have for another ten years if she was careful. But then Wendy was out in the hot sun and the cold winds all year round and it showed in her face.

The daughter had to be late teens, which would make the mother older than she looked. Unless she had had the child at an uncommonly early age, in which case.... It was no use trying to figure it out because he'd probably come up with the wrong answer. He'd ask the daughter her age at the first opportunity, which shouldn't offend anyone, should it? And if he knew the daughter's age, it shouldn't be all that difficult to calculate the mother's.

The daughter was the one who looked like a New Yorker, with all that makeup on her face and the kind of short, spiky hairdo that he had heard about, no doubt seen pictures of, but which wasn't a haircut that had gained any popularity in Wyoming from what he had seen.

Other than the hairdo and the makeup and the fact that her face was a little rounder, a little less formed, she was a dead ringer for the mother. They both had long, slim legs, almost no hips, and enough in the bosom department to be feminine without being blatant about it. Dolly Parton they weren't. They both had the same color hair, which he had always heard called towhead when it was on little kids, but which, on the mother, was such a silvery blond that it looked like moonlight. Hers was long and perfectly straight, parted on the side with a few strands shorter and falling diagonally across her forehead. They both had small, straight noses, green eyes the shade of olives, wide mouths, and the mother had a few freckles on her nose and across her cheeks. She wore no makeup at all that he could discern, and with her kind of beauty it would have been a desecration. They both had perfect, golden tans, too, although how they got those tans in New York he didn't know.

And here he was, sitting in their car and practically drawing a picture of her in his head. It must have been that the hospital stay had softened his brain. He might be in the market for a partner in life, but he didn't have to go outside of Wyoming to find one, and he sure as hell didn't have to pick up one on the road. And while he wasn't looking for some amenable country girl, he also wasn't looking for some argumentative, know-it-all New York type to whom bossing men was probably second nature.

And for that matter, he wasn't looking all *that* hard or he probably would've found someone by now.

Still, he couldn't quite shake off the scenario. He could picture the woman driving while he stretched out in the seat beside her, leaving those funny little seats in the back for the kid. He might even be able to do some of his leg exercises in the confined space, and there was always the possibility—although even in his imagination this possibility didn't seem all that possible—that at night, when they stopped at some motel, he could get the woman to help him with his leg exercises in the same way the physical therapist in the hospital had helped him. It wouldn't be half bad having that woman grabbing hold of his foot and his calf while he slowly, ever so slowly, retrained his knee to bend.

It wasn't like he had to get back to the ranch in a hurry. The time factor was no problem at all. He'd be out of commission for the next few months anyway, and Wendy could handle the ranch on her own. In fact, Wendy would probably thank him for not showing up so soon; he'd only get in her way, the condition he was in. She'd feel she had to fuss over him instead of running the ranch.

Oh, hell, who was he kidding this time? Wendy fuss over him? Hell, that'd be the day.

Yeah, he was decided; it was the only way to go. He could certainly argue that they owed him a ride, and he owed it to his leg to let them. Still, the decision was going to be up to them.

He wasn't thrilled about the fact they were New Yorkers. He had had more than enough of New Yorkers in the hospital to last him a lifetime. He'd had enough of New York *drivers* to last him an eternity. Trying to get out of the city had been like trying to drive a cow through a herd of bulls.

He saw the door to the state troopers' building open and the kid come out. She came down the steps and headed right for him and he reached out and opened the window on the passenger side. She leaned down, rested her arms on the car door and looked inside at him. She looked like she had even more makeup on than before, and he had the feeling it was for the benefit of those two kids in uniform who had driven them into town.

"I was starting to get worried about you," she said.

"Afraid I might have stolen your car?" Billy asked her, wondering if she was the usual paranoid New Yorker.

She grinned at him. "Steal it, go on, you have my permission. I don't know why Mom couldn't have gotten a regular car, a comfortable one. I think she sees herself as some kind of adventurer driving this car."

"It's an adventure, all right," agreed Billy.

"I was worried maybe the drive was too much for you. You looked pretty shaky on your crutches back there."

Billy, who didn't want to come across as a sniveling complainer, ignored this and asked, "What's happening inside? I take it no one's getting locked up in the hoosegow."

Her eyes began to glimmer. "The *what*?"

"The jail. I thought maybe that trooper had taken such a liking to you he threw you in and kept the key."

"You mean Daryl," she said, and he was kind of sorry that everyone seemed to be on a first-name basis except him.

"I guess I better come in and give the car-rental place a call," said Billy, taking the keys out of the ignition and handing them to her, then opening the door, grabbing his crutches and staggering out of the car. He almost fell right there in the street, but instead propelled himself back against the car until he got his balance.

He saw her watching him, her smooth forehead puckering up into a frown. "You need some help?" she asked.

"Cowboys don't like to ask for help," said Billy, saying it in a joking manner but knowing, deep down, that it was the doggoned truth. Asking women for help was like asking a steer to stand still while you branded him.

She kept a watchful eye on him as he headed around the car and made for the stairs. There were only five of them, and there was a wooden railing leading up, but just the sight of the stairs was enough to make the sweat break out on his forehead. He had been trained on the stairs in the hospital, but that had been with a walker and it hadn't been one of his more glorious moments. He had sworn up and down to the therapist that there were no stairs at home and that was something that could wait until he got his leg more in control.

And now five tiny little stairs were going to make the difference between looking like a totally-in-control cowboy and a helpless jackass.

He stood there for a moment assessing them. He figured the way to go about it would be to transfer his right crutch into his left hand, grab onto the railing with his right and try to hoist himself up step by step.

With the left crutch firmly under his arm, he transferred the other crutch to his left hand, only his left hand suddenly became afraid to let go of his left crutch and the other crutch fell down onto the sidewalk with a clatter. He quickly grabbed hold of the railing with his right hand.

Acting like he didn't even care about that crutch down on the ground, acting like he had meant it to fall on the ground, Billy studiously avoided even looking at it. He saw the girl reach down and pick it up for him, though, not making any big deal out of it, which made him feel a little better.

Billy put half his weight on the remaining crutch and half his weight on the railing and tried to lift his entire body onto the first step. For some reason his upper body seemed to have lost its strength, because very little happened, and his body barely moved. And he could see very clearly that there was no way he was going to get up those stairs on his own and equally no way he was going to ask for help.

"You know what you could do," said the girl, sitting down on the stairs but leaving him room to maneuver, "you could go up those stairs like little kids do. You know, sitting down on one and then pushing with your hands and sitting on the next until you're all the way to the top."

Billy got the picture. It sounded like a totally good idea except that if anyone walked by he'd feel really stupid. But then maybe it was about time he started getting used to feeling really stupid. He wasn't in the hospital anymore, where just about everyone was looking equally stupid. He was out in the real world, and he was going to have to get used to people looking at him. He was a sight to see, that's all.

Grateful it was only the girl seeing him and not the troopers, and especially not her mother, Billy turned around and sat down on the second-to-bottom stair. Without saying a word, the girl took the other crutch from him.

Using his hands, Billy made it to the next step. He gave a bump to his knee along the way, and the sudden pain would have been enough to make him cry out if he'd still been in the hospital where it was all right to cry out. Instead, he pressed his lips very tightly together and hoped to hell he wouldn't pass out.

Two more steps, that was all, and he made them without giving his knee another bump. But now he was at the top of the stairs, and he wasn't at all sure he could pull himself upright.

"What a hassle," said the girl, hunkering down next to him. "You're making me worried I'm going to break a leg skiing. I'd sure hate to be in a cast for six months and trying to get along on crutches like you're doing. I think it was pretty brave of you to even try to drive a car."

Ah, what balm to his ego. Maybe he'd forget about the mother; this girl was sure a doll. Maybe he'd just bypass the mother and adopt the girl.

"You do much skiing in New York City?" Billy asked her, thinking a little conversation would give him a much-

needed rest before the big attempt to get up and fall flat
on his face.

She chuckled. "No, I've done all my skiing in Vermont, which is why I'm really looking forward to Colorado."

"You're headed for Colorado?" asked Billy, which seemed propitious, Colorado being right next door to Wyoming.

She nodded.

"I don't think skiing season's quite started there yet," he said, "although sometimes August'll fool you and some snow will come out of nowhere."

"I'm going to college there."

"That right?" said Billy, the pieces of the scenario suddenly beginning to fit together perfectly.

"Yes. Mom's driving me to college." She straightened up and looked down at him. "If you could swing your legs over onto the porch, I could probably pull you upright." And then, without even waiting or offering to help, she leaned down and gently moved his legs up onto the porch, not even jarring them a little.

Billy sighed in relief. He hadn't the least idea how he was going to get back down the stairs, though.

She reached down her hands and he took them, trusting her not to let go all of a sudden and send him falling back down the stairs. She had strength in her arms and with just a little effort had him standing upright. She took his hands and placed them on the railing, then picked up his crutches and helped him place them beneath his arms.

Then she opened the door for him and held it while he was able to walk through it and into the police station with more dignity than he deserved. Hell, if it hadn't been for her he might be crawling inside right now.

"You're doing fine," she whispered to him as they entered the station side by side. And then it was anticlimactic because no one was even looking at them.

The trooper with the red hair was at an antiquated typewriter filling in some form. The woman was on the phone, one hand going to her hair and brushing it out of her eyes, her mouth twisted up in a way that signaled to him she wasn't hearing good news from the other end. The blond trooper had eyes only for the girl.

"All right if I use your phone to call the car-rental agency in New York?" he asked the blond trooper.

Billy was waved to a phone and was about to pick it up when the woman put her hand over the mouthpiece of her phone and said to him, "My insurance agent wants to know where you rented the car. They'll take care of notifying them."

"It was a Hertz place," said Billy, "but I don't rightly know which one. They delivered it to the hospital."

She spoke the words "Hertz" and "Manhattan" into the phone, listened for a moment, then turned to Billy. "They need to know the date, your name and your driver's license number."

"Day before yesterday, whatever that was," said Billy. "William Blue's the name and I can't give you the number on my driver's license because I never thought to memorize it and it went up in smoke along with the car."

"Daryl," the girl was saying to the blond trooper, "is there somewhere around here I could get some coffee?"

"There's a restaurant down the block a ways," said the trooper. "Maybe you should get us all coffee; we're going to be here for a while."

"Anything I got to do or sign around here?" asked Billy.

The trooper shook his head. "Not unless you're planning on filing charges of some kind."

There was dead silence in the room for a moment, and then Billy said, "No charges. I'll let Hertz fight it out with the insurance company."

The girl was heading for the door when Billy said, "Hold on, I'll walk down there with you."

She gave him a look as good as saying "Do you think you ought to?" but Billy figured he'd much rather try getting down those stairs now, when only the girl would see him, rather than later, with everyone there to watch.

It was easier going down. Billy used the railing and one crutch, and the girl stood in front of him as though to break his fall in case of a mishap.

"Hey, you did that all right, William," she said when he got to the bottom.

"William? No one's ever called me William," he said. "My name's Billy Blue."

"I like that much better," she said. "William didn't sound much like a cowboy. You are a cowboy, aren't you?"

"I guess you'd say I'm a rancher," said Billy, but he always liked thinking of himself as a cowboy. And hell, if he wasn't a cowboy, who was? "I don't believe I know your name."

"I'm Melissa Allman, but I'm usually called Mouse. What'd you do to your knee?" asked Mouse, with the frankness kids always had.

"Got it crushed under a horse."

That got a look of admiration from her. Well, hell, didn't she think cowboys still used horses? Not that he and Wendy didn't have their own four-wheel drive back at the ranch, and theirs was a real, working one.

The few people in town were giving them a wide berth on the sidewalk. They were eyeing the girl's haircut and his leg and Stetson, and he figured they were adding a little novelty to their small-town life.

"Sorry to get you all the way up those stairs," said Mouse. "I guess you could've waited in the car."

"You didn't know that," said Billy. "I figured the police would want me to fill out all kinds of forms."

"I think it's Mom who's going to have to do that. Me, too, I guess, since I was the criminal. Thanks for not pressing charges. Or suing me or anything."

"What would be the point?"

"I don't know, but a New Yorker would've."

"That's what comes of living in the big, bad city," said Billy. "Where I come from people help each other out." And what was he now, some self-appointed Chamber of Commerce spokesperson for Wyoming? When it came right down to it, this girl—Mouse—was probably nicer and more helpful than anyone back home would be, and that included Wendy who was so self-sufficient and independent herself she expected everyone else to be the same.

Billy slowed down and came to a stop.

"You okay?" asked Mouse.

"I could use a pain pill," Billy admitted.

"I forgot, your pain pills went over with your car, right?"

"Hell, honey I had an entire pharmacy with me. I guess what I'm going to have to do is stop at a drugstore here and have them call my doctor in New York."

"We'll get you seated at the restaurant and then I'll find out where a pharmacy is."

He thought he was strong. He was sure he wasn't one of those weaklings like the ones who lived in cities. But not only was his knee hurting, but his underarms and also his wrists. Six weeks in the hospital seemed to have drained him of all his strength.

He started out again, putting all of his weight on his right leg and just swinging his left along in the air. He began to break out in a cold sweat and he fought the dizziness he was feeling. Here he was, dressed like some relic of the old west—at least to the people in this part of the country—and he was in danger of fainting dead away on their sidewalk. It wasn't an appealing thought.

The girl moved in close to him and put an arm around his waist. "Just lean on me, okay? If you want, you can hand me one of your crutches and put your arm around my shoulder."

"I just might take you up on that," said Billy, his last vestige of machismo melting away.

She took his crutch, and he balanced himself instead with his arm around her neck and he wondered how in hell he was going to make it back to the police station.

A few more steps and Mouse said, "We're here now," and handed him back his crutch and opened the door for him.

After the late morning sun on the street, the interior seemed dark until Billy realized he was still wearing his sunglasses. But since they were prescription sunglasses, and since without them he couldn't see any farther than his nose, and since being half blind plus a cripple was a little more than he could handle at the moment, he left them on.

"Sit down here," Mouse was saying to him, pulling out a chair at one of the tables. "I'll see if they'll give me some aspirin and a glass of water, and if you want to order some food, I'll wait with you."

"You better get back or your mom might worry about you taking off with a strange man."

"I'm an adult," he was informed.

"And how old might that be?"

"I was eighteen last month."

"Yeah, that's adult," said Billy, remembering feeling exactly the same way the first time he could walk into a bar and get served legally. Of course, the drinking laws had since changed.

Billy took off his hat and fanned his face with it as his eyes adjusted to the lighting. He could now see about a half dozen other tables, a few stools at a counter and a blackboard listing the day's specials. He'd have some strong coffee to get him going again and maybe a hamburger or two.

Mouse came back with a waitress who was carrying a glass of water and a bottle of Extra Strength Tylenol she set in front of him. The waitress didn't look much older than Mouse, and she was eyeing him with curiosity. *The crippled cowboy, line up for the sideshow,* he was thinking to himself as he opened the bottle, shook out a few of the tablets and downed them. Which meant he'd need at least two cups of coffee to offset the drowsy effect the pills would produce, and another two just to keep him going.

"Mighty obliged for the painkillers," he told the waitress. "I'll have me a pot of coffee and a couple of burgers, rare. What about you, Mouse, can I get you anything?"

"I'm just going to get coffee to go for now; I'll wait for Mom." She turned to the waitress, "A Coke and three coffees to go with cream and sugar on the side."

When the waitress left, Billy said, "Pretty nice of your mom to drive you a couple thousand miles to college."

Mouse looked doubtful. "I have my own suspicions about that. I think she's going to look for a job out there and move in on me. I don't think she wants me leaving home."

Billy thought of his own mother, who two weeks after he and his sister had gone off to school, had taken a job as a game warden because she said the house was so quiet it was driving her nuts. "I guess that's natural," he said. "Unlike wildlife, humans don't always like to see their children leave the nest."

"We're really close."

"That's nice," said Billy.

"Sometimes I think we're *too* close." She slid down into one of the chairs and leaned toward him across the table. "I feel I need my own space."

Billy, who had never lacked for space in his lightly inhabited area of the state, nodded in understanding. "What about your dad?"

"You know what hippies are?"

"Sure, we even had some in Wyoming once upon a time," said Billy.

"Well, Mom says my dad is one of the last of them. The last we heard—which was years ago, I wasn't even in school yet—was that he was living in some cave on Crete. That's a Greek island."

"I've heard of Crete, too."

"I think what Mom needs is a man. I mean, she didn't need one before because she had me, but now she's going to be all alone."

Billy couldn't think of a thing to say to that, and then he was suddenly made uncomfortably aware that Mouse was eyeing him speculatively. He might have the idea in his own head, but he didn't take kindly to others pushing ideas off on him. He'd had more of matchmaking than he could stomach, and a sure way to put him off was to push someone in his direction.

"How old are you, Billy?" she asked him.

"Thirty-six."

"Oh, well," she said, shrugging, obviously dismissing him as a potential man in her mother's life.

Good. No matchmaking. That made it all right for him to move ahead on his own. "How old's your mom?" he asked, trying to sound just casually interested.

"She'll be thirty-eight in a couple of months, but she lies about her age."

"I can see where she could get away with that," observed Billy.

"She says she's forty-two. It all started when she was young and trying to get a job. She says employers took her more seriously when she said she was older."

Billy couldn't remember lying about his age since he was sixteen and trying to get served. It had never worked because he had always looked young for his age in those days. Now he supposed he looked his age, no better or no worse. In fact, the only times he even thought about his age were on those occasions when his mother pointed it out to him, and that was usually followed by the question of when he was planning on tying the knot. Despite her own questionable marriage, his mother was a firm believer in the institution, and the fact that Wendy and he hadn't was a thorn in her side. No, not a thorn in her side—more like a buzzsaw in her mouth.

"What're you going to do now," said Mouse, "rent another car?"

"Going to be a little difficult what with my credit cards and money and driver's license burnt up like that."

"I don't know how you drove anyway," said Mouse. "You can barely walk."

Billy grinned at her honesty. None of that polite talk out of her, like the nurses in the hospital who would say, "Oh, aren't we doing well today," when in actuality he was barely making it to the john on his own.

"I figure it's got to get better every day," said Billy. "The trouble is, my leg gets stiff being in one position all day."

"You'd probably be better off in the back seat with someone else driving."

Billy nodded. "Probably," he said, seeing the direction in which her mind was drifting.

"Not in our car, though," mused Mouse. "Our back seat is pretty useless."

"That a fact?" asked Billy.

"Well, it's not completely useless. I mean I could sit in it, or even Mom, but someone...well, someone as tall as you would be pretty uncomfortable. And there'd be no room to stretch out your leg."

"No place for a cripple, I reckon."

"But the passenger seat wouldn't be bad," said Mouse, which almost made Billy believe in ESP, as he'd been rather hoping that would occur to her. "How far is Wyoming from Colorado? I know I should know that without asking, but geography isn't one of my strong points."

"Hell, they rub right up against each other," said Billy. "Just like New York and New Jersey."

"I think we owe you a ride home."

Billy let that thought settle between them for a moment until it took on substance. "I wouldn't want to be a burden."

"The thing is, you were probably trying to overdo it, get home too fast. We're just taking our time and seeing the sights. We stop pretty early every day and look for a motel."

"Lots of sights to see between here and Colorado?"

Mouse grinned. "To tell you the truth, your car going over the cliff was the most exciting thing I've seen so far."

"Kind of satisfying to know I added to your enjoyment of the scenery."

"I think the least we can do is give you a ride home. And I'm sure Mom will agree, too," she added, but not sounding nearly as sure as her words would have him believe.

"Well, I guess it would solve one of my problems," said Billy, trying not to sound too eager.

"It'd be fun to have you along," said Mouse. "Mom and I get to talk all the time, so it gets kind of boring after a while. It would be interesting to have a new person to talk to."

"I'll provide the entertainment," said Billy.

She laughed out loud. "I didn't mean that."

"Hey, I can be real entertaining at times. You ought to hear me around a camp fire."

Mouse gave him a doubtful look, as well she might. She was a smart New York City girl, not some gullible kid from the boonies.

The waitress brought his coffee and hamburgers to the table, along with two bags to go. "Well, go to it," Billy said to Mouse. "Go sell your mom on the idea of helping out a poor crippled cowboy who can barely drive a car."

Mouse's mouth pursed. "I know you think you're kidding, Billy, but it's the truth. You really don't look as though you ought to be taking care of yourself. I bet you haven't been out of the hospital a week."

"Two days," said Billy, between bites of his burger.

Mouse stood up. "Okay, I'll give it my best shot. In any case, I'll stop by and let you know the answer, and Mom will probably have to talk to you about your car."

And then she was gone and Billy belatedly realized that he was running up a bill and didn't have one cent in his pockets, and if Mouse and her mother didn't return, the troopers would have every reason in the world to throw him in jail this time.

He had sure sunk low in the world.

Chapter Three

Mouse backed slowly through the door of the police station, trying to balance the four containers without spilling them, while at the same time attempting to maintain the look of a sophisticated New Yorker who just happened to be passing through town.

She saw almost the exact tableau as when she had left: her mother was still on the phone and still looking angry; Chris was still at the typewriter filling out forms; and Daryl, now that he saw her, was grinning at her again, just the way he had when she said she'd go get them some coffee. The cowboy was pretty cute, but Daryl was serious stuff. Daryl didn't look like any of the boys she had gone to high school with, although it might be partly the uniform. The uniform was pretty sexy. But mostly it was his big mouth that appealed to her. She had somewhat of a big mouth herself and could verbally demolish most of the boys she met. Daryl, though, didn't appear to be someone she could demolish. She thought they were pretty even on that score.

Mouse said, "I'm back," and Chris stopped typing and her mother, with a final, sarcastic, "Thank you for your caring attitude," slammed down the phone.

Mouse eyed her mother warily as she handed her the Coke. Suzanne was looking like she was wondering what she was doing in this hick police station in this hick town. Mouse had a feeling they were going to be back in New York in a matter of hours. Her mother was a city person. Her mother was never going to be able to survive out here in the boondocks. One major disaster—and Mouse guessed this was a major disaster—and she figured her mother would head back to the safety of the city.

The place wasn't much as far as police stations went, although Mouse hadn't actually been in one before. It just didn't look much like the police stations on TV shows. There was a counter, and behind the counter, where they were, were only a couple of desks and uncomfortable chairs and some metal file cabinets and a calendar on the wall with a picture of a half-naked girl. In a separate office, about the size of a closet, was a woman who manned the radio. The woman had poked out her curly gray head once, yelled for them to keep the noise down and then retreated to her office.

Mouse's eyes kept going to the calendar. She watched Daryl to see if he looked at it, but he and Chris seemed to ignore it. Mouse had trouble ignoring it. She found it pretty embarrassing to be in the same room with a picture of a topless woman. A woman who was very large in the exact area where she was topless. If Daryl had spent his time staring at the topless woman, Mouse would have found that a turnoff, but so far she hadn't seen him even look at it once.

Daryl raised his cup of coffee to Mouse. "You found the place all right?"

Mouse said, "This town isn't big enough to get lost in." Daryl looked a little annoyed at that, so Mouse added, "It looks like a really nice place, though. Quiet;

kind of peaceful." All true, but all adding up to boring. She hadn't even seen a movie theater.

"I don't care what your sign says," Suzanne was saying. "I'm lighting a cigarette, and if you want to arrest me for it, that's up to you."

"Go ahead," said Chris. "No one ever pays any attention to that sign," and then he looked surprised when Suzanne looked furious at the news. Knowing her mom, she could have smoked half a pack in the time she was away getting them coffee.

"What'd the insurance man say?" Mouse asked her mother.

"Oh, we're covered. My insurance premium will probably skyrocket next year, and they were slightly annoyed that we completely destroyed a car only a week after the policy went into effect, but they're contacting Hertz and taking care of everything."

"What about Billy?" asked Mouse.

"Billy?"

"Billy Blue, the cowboy. Are they going to send him another car?"

Daryl said, "I expect he'll have to go to Cleveland to pick up another rental. We don't have any car-rental agencies in town, and I've never heard of them delivering them this distance."

"What about us?" Mouse asked her mother.

"What do you mean?"

"I mean, are you still driving me to college?"

"Of course. I might take over most of the driving, though."

Mouse tried to hide her excitement. "You mean we don't have to go back to New York?"

"Why in the world would we go back to New York?"

"I don't know," said Mouse, wondering how she could have read her mother's mood so wrong.

Suzanne stood up and stretched. "What I could use, Mouse, is some lunch. That restaurant you just went to, did it look all right?"

"It was fine," said Mouse, thinking it no better nor worse than the coffee shops in New York.

"Best restaurant in town," said Daryl.

"That was the *best*?" said Mouse.

"Good home-cooked food, just the way your mom cooks it," said Daryl, a gleam in his eyes.

Mouse wasn't going to touch that one with a ten-foot pole. Suzanne's idea of cooking was ordering in Chinese and warming it up in the microwave. She had been known to joke that the only thing she could cook was sushi.

"*Only* restaurant in town," said Chris, pulling a form out of the typewriter and approaching Suzanne with it. "If you'll just sign here, ma'am. All four copies."

"Six hundred dollars?" questioned Suzanne, reading the spaces filled in on the form.

"Ma'am, right now an emergency repair crew is out there fixing the guardrail, and a towing service from the next town over is going to contract to bring up what's left of that car your daughter wrecked."

"Can't you just leave it there?"

"Ma'am, this isn't New York City. When people stop at that lookout point they don't want to see junk when they look down. They want to look at the God-given beauty of nature. This is Ohio—we're proud of our scenery."

"Well put, Chris," said Daryl, looking over at Mouse with a grin.

Suzanne sighed deeply before signing all four copies. "Do you take credit cards?" she asked.

"No, ma'am."

Another sigh. "Traveler's checks?"

"Yes, ma'am, that'd be just fine."

Everyone stood around watching as Suzanne signed six hundred dollars worth of twenty-dollar traveler's checks. When she was finished, she handed the checks to Chris and stood up. "You know where this restaurant is, Mouse?"

"Yes, ma'am," said Mouse, then started to laugh at the expression on her mom's face. "I meant *Mom*. Sorry. I guess it's catching."

"Is there a ladies' room here?"

"It's right down the hall, Mom. It just says toilet, but I guess anyone can use it."

As soon as her mom headed down the hall, Daryl said, "If you're still in Maple Grove tonight, you want to go out?"

Mouse figured she didn't have time to play hard to get. Anyway, she definitely wanted to go out with him. He was just about the cutest guy she had ever seen. And older, too, at least twenty, twenty-one. "Sure, if I'm still around," she said.

Daryl said, "I'll give you a call later, then."

"How will you know where to call me?"

Daryl grinned. "There's only one motel in town."

Now that the date was ensured, Mouse got a little more reckless. "Not that there looks like much to do in this hick town," she said, throwing a taunting look Daryl's way.

"Oh, hell, no," said Daryl, getting into it. "Not even a subway in town where we could go for a ride and get mugged."

Mouse began to warm up. "I guess we could always go out and count the trees along the highway. That could make for a pretty exciting evening."

"You spotted that, did you?" asked Daryl. "Yeah, that's one of the major attractions around here. That and watching the tourists go over the lookout point."

"Now in New York," said Mouse, "we'd have a choice. We could go to a movie, or maybe a Broadway show, or if that sounded too boring we could always go to Madison Square Garden to a rock concert."

"Oh, yeah, rocks," said Daryl. "Sometimes we go down by the river at night and throw rocks in the water. That's usually not on a first date, though. I usually save that up for someone I'm serious about. And if I'm really serious, we even pack a picnic to take along. And then when the mosquitoes come out and start to swarm, we feed them."

Her mom returned before Mouse could get another dig in, and Mouse ushered her out the door. Halfway down the block she broached the subject. "Did you know Billy just got out of the hospital a couple days ago?"

"Since I only met Billy briefly, I would hardly know that, Mouse. Nor does it interest me. Not that I'm not sorry for the predicament we've put him in."

"I put him in it, not you."

"Not true, Mouse; I allowed you to drive."

"Listen, Mom, the poor guy's having trouble driving."

"I expect he's going to have even more trouble driving without a car," said Suzanne.

"Very funny. I knock a poor cripple's car over a cliff and you make jokes about it. I can't believe this is the exact same mother who was always giving change to the homeless. That and cigarettes, which wasn't doing them any favors."

"I don't quite see the connection between the victim of a car accident and the homeless in New York."

"Billy's worse than homeless, Mom. He's on the highway without a car. I hope he knows how to hitchhike."

"Well, Mouse, I wasn't planning on just leaving him here. Of course we'll drive him to the nearest car-rental agency, even if it's all the way to Cleveland. But not today. For some reason I've had just about enough of traveling today."

"Great," said Mouse, thinking how pleased Daryl would be when he found out she was spending the night in town.

Suzanne instantly became suspicious. "You don't mind stopping for the day?"

"Not at all. Not that this town looks like a whole lot of fun, but I think Billy needs to rest. You know something? He just got out of the hospital two days ago."

"Yes, I believe you just mentioned that. Well, that's fine. We'll all get a much-needed rest."

"Be nice to him, okay, Mom? He's really a sweet guy."

"Of course I'll be nice to him. My daughter totaled his car, do you think I'm going to go out of my way to be rude? He could probably have us arrested."

When they entered the restaurant, Billy was eating a big piece of pie with a scoop of ice cream on top, and Mouse could see the waitress hovering nearby. The restaurant had a few other customers but it wasn't anything like a lunch-hour crowd in New York. Mouse had a feeling the waitress was flirting with Billy. They probably didn't get many cowboys for customers and cowboys, at least in the movies, were always wonderfully romantic characters.

Mouse headed straight for Billy's table and sat down next to him, not giving her mother a chance to choose another table and make things difficult.

"How'd it go?" Billy asked when Suzanne sat down across from him.

"They fined me six hundred dollars."

"That's a lot of money," said Billy. "You going to be able to manage that?"

Suzanne nodded. "I wrote them out some traveler's checks."

"This is real embarrassing," said Billy, lowering his voice, "but the fact of the matter is, my wallet went over the cliff with my car, and I'm right now running up a check with no money to pay for it."

"Mom will pay for it, Billy," said Mouse.

Billy grinned at Suzanne. "Is that right, Mom?"

Suzanne rolled her eyes, as though dealing with two teenagers. "Do you have any way to get some money?"

Billy nodded. "I'll call home and they'll wire me some. I'm just not going to get it in time to pay this check unless I spend the next few hours sitting here ordering food."

"This is on me," said Suzanne. "And we'll also put you up in a motel room for the night. Then tomorrow I'll drive you to Cleveland to your car-rental agency. They said to tell you you could pick up another car at the next agency you come to."

"That's decent of you, ma'am," said Billy.

"Is that okay, Billy?" asked Mouse. "We decided not to start out again today."

"Fine with me," said Billy. "I'll be lucky at this point if I can make it to a bed."

Mouse noticed movement to her left and saw the waitress creeping toward their table. The woman's eyes were on her mother and they were as wide as a six-lane highway. Oh, no, thought Mouse, realizing that Suzanne had been recognized. It had happened at a gas station the day before, surprising the hell out of both of them.

The waitress came right up to the table and sat down in the empty chair. Ignoring everyone else, she looked into Suzanne's eyes and said, "Barbara Jean, I knew it was you."

Probably not even realizing she was doing it, her mom's face took on the sweet, rather dumb expression of Barbara Jean.

"Why, honey," said the waitress, "I was so upset when I heard you were leaving town. I said to my sister, Marilyn, 'You can't blame her for wanting out of there.' I mean, there's only so much you ought to have to take, and Victor dumping on you the way he did, well, that was the last straw. And after all you went through for him, too."

Mouse saw Billy looking amazed at what was going on. She didn't know whether to explain or not but thought she better leave it up to her mom, who usually got annoyed when Mouse told anyone what she did for a living.

The waitress was saying, "What would you like to eat, Barbara Jean? You just name it, it'll be a real pleasure serving you."

"I think a hamburger, medium rare, and a Coke."

"I'll have a burger, too," said Mouse, "and another cup of coffee," but the waitress ignored her, her eyes never leaving Suzanne.

"You just wait until I tell Kitty you're out here," said the waitress. "She's the cook, and she's going to want to come out and say hello to you personally, I just know. Why, this is just like a miracle happening in our restaurant."

There was rather a lengthy silence at the table when the waitress left. Suzanne was looking off into the distance, Billy was staring at Suzanne, and Mouse was trying to think of something to say to break the silence.

It was Billy who finally said, "You been here before, Barbara Jean?"

"My name isn't Barbara Jean," said her mom.

Billy said, "I could've sworn that's what Cindi called you."

"Cindi?" said Mouse. "You know the waitress's name?"

"We got to talking after you left. Real friendly girl. Course nothing to how friendly she was to Barbara Jean here."

"Billy, this is my mom, Suzanne. Mom, this is Billy Blue, isn't that a great name?"

Neither of them said a word and they were still sitting there in silence when Cindi came back with the drinks. She hovered around the table for a few moments, her eyes on Suzanne, then drifted back to the counter.

"Someone going to solve the mystery for me?" asked Billy.

Mouse changed the subject. "What exactly's wrong with your leg, Billy?"

Billy gave her a look that said he knew she was weaseling out of answering his question, and Mouse had the feeling he didn't like talking about his leg any more than her mother liked talking about Barbara Jean, but when you walked around with crutches you had to expect a few questions.

"My horse fell on me and crushed the hell out of my knee. Got a whole new knee replacement put in in New York. Plastic over titanium—supposed to be better than the real thing."

Suzanne looked interested. "Knees. That's supposed to be painful. Half the runners I know in New York seem to be having knee operations."

"You know a lot of runners?" asked Billy.

"I know a lot of people who run," said Suzanne.

Mouse said, "Everyone runs in New York, Billy. Not me, but just about everyone else. Mom ran in the marathon last year."

"Did you win?" Billy asked Suzanne.

Suzanne gave him her sincere "Barbara Jean" look. "Of course. I finished in one hour and fifty-five minutes."

"That's a long time to run," said Billy, but Mouse didn't think he was really taken in because his eyes had a spark to them.

"She's lying," said Mouse. "You got to watch her, if she looks really sincere when she says something, you can bet it's an all-out lie. No one finishes the marathon in that time. Mom was lucky to cross the finish line."

"You folks know about a motel in town?" asked Billy.

Suzanne nodded. "The troopers told us about one. The only one in town, it seems."

"I'm sure it'll be fine," said Mouse, who so far had liked what she'd seen of motels. The one last night had had a live band playing in the lounge and the drummer had smiled at her a couple of times.

"I wouldn't count on it," said Suzanne. "This doesn't seem to be our lucky day."

"Oh, now, don't say that, Barbara Jean," said the waitress, coming up behind them with the hamburgers.

"You got to think positive, honey, if you want to find happiness. Maybe leaving town was the best thing you ever did."

THE WOMAN IN THE MOTEL office said, "Well, now, you must be the folks had the accident at the lookout point. The troopers said you might be stopping by. Said I should take good care of you folks."

She pushed a registration card over to Billy and another one to Suzanne, then reached into her pocket and put on a pair of glasses. Then she looked up and got a good look at Suzanne.

"Oh, lordy," she screamed, her hands going to the sides of her face. "It's Barbara Jean, isn't it? Right here in my motel. Whoever would've thought! Ma'am, could I bother you to sign an autograph for me? Just here, on the back of this pad will do."

"Will someone please tell me—" Billy started to say, but Mouse elbowed him in the ribs to shut him up.

The motel was built in an L shape around a small swimming pool. They were given rooms next to each other on the ground floor, in deference to Billy's crutches. The rooms were clean and cheerful with a color TV and a view of the pool.

They were still unpacking when Billy knocked on their door. When Mouse opened it, Billy looked past her to her mother and said, "If you could do me a favor, ma'am, I'd be much obliged."

"If people don't stop calling me ma'am," said Suzanne, "I'm going to scream."

"Only being polite, Barbara Jean, honey," said Billy, trying on a grin even though Mouse could see he was in pain.

"You looking to walk to Cleveland?" Suzanne asked him.

"Your mom's a hard woman," Billy said to Mouse.

"What's the favor, Billy?" asked Mouse.

"I got hold of the hospital in New York and my prescriptions are being called in to the pharmacy in town. I also called home and some money's being wired to me here."

"Don't worry," said Mouse, "we'll pick up what you need at the pharmacy. You just rest that leg this afternoon."

Billy waited for confirmation from Suzanne, who finally said, "Just write down anything else you might need and we'll get it for you."

"I'll go make a list," said Billy, "and I'm much obliged, ma'am."

"Let's get one thing straight, Billy," said Suzanne. "The martyr act has got to go. No more being obliged and no more ma'ams. Are we clear on that?"

"I was never too good asking favors of folks."

"Obviously," said Suzanne.

"Well, all right," said Billy. "You folks can pick up my list on your way out."

"You're awfully hard on him," said Mouse when she heard the door to Billy's room close.

"I'm not used to people being that polite all the time; it makes me nervous."

"Can we go swimming when we get back?"

"That's another thing, Mouse—you're eighteen now, you're going to be on your own at college, if we ever get you there. You don't have to ask my permission to do everything. If you want to swim, swim. If you want to go out with that blond trooper tonight, go."

"You knew about that?" asked Mouse.

"I'm not blind."

Mouse was beginning to see that being eighteen had a lot of advantages.

When they were leaving, Mouse stopped by for Billy's list. He was lying on the bed with his head propped up on the pillows. He handed her the list and she looked it over.

"Are you sure this is all you need?" she asked him.

"Well, I'm going to need a few clothes and some shaving stuff, but that can wait until my money arrives. You could pick me out something to read, though, if they have books there."

Mouse looked around to make sure her mother wasn't behind her, then said, "Listen, Billy. At two-thirty, turn on the TV. I don't know what channel it is here, but it's ABC."

"And what am I going to see?"

Mouse grinned. "It's called *Reach for the Sky*."

"That sounds to me like one of those soap operas."

"It is. But you're going to love this one, Billy, I promise. Just don't tell anyone I told you, okay?"

"As long as you don't tell anyone I watch soap operas."

THE FIRST THINGS her mom bought in the drugstore were a pair of sunglasses and a bright blue baseball cap. With the sunglasses over her eyes and her hair pushed up under the cap, no one appeared to recognize her as Barbara Jean.

"Good disguise, Mom," said Mouse.

"I can't believe all this recognition," said her mom. "These people sure aren't like New Yorkers. If people acted like that in New York, I would have quit the show years ago."

"I think it's kind of sweet. You're probably the most exciting thing that's happened to this town in years."

"That and ruining their lookout point. Is this enough? Would you recognize me?"

"Sure, but I don't think your fans will. I think they recognize you by your hair and your eyes; now you just look like the average tourist."

"Just what I've always aspired to," muttered Suzanne.

Mouse looked at the magazines and books while they waited for the prescriptions to be filled.

"You finished all your books already?" asked Suzanne.

"I'm getting something for Billy. He's out of everything, Mom. No clothes, no shaving stuff, no nothing."

"He didn't put any of that on his list."

"I think he wanted to wait until he got his own money."

"I'll take him shopping tonight."

"You will?" said Mouse, having thought that was something she'd have to talk her mom into.

"I don't mind. It beats sitting around the motel."

"What do you think Billy would read?"

"Get him a Western. He looks like he'd enjoy a Western."

"I don't think so," said Mouse, picking out one of Stephen King's books. "I think he could probably *write* a Western."

Using her own money, she bought Billy a bag of goodies. There was the King book; a couple of news magazines in case he hadn't kept in touch with the world while he was in the hospital; assorted candy bars and gum; a comb and a toothbrush and some toothpaste; a package of disposable razors and some Noxema shaving lotion; and a T-shirt with a map of Ohio on it.

Her mother saw her paying for the stuff at the counter and asked her if she wanted some money.

"No. I want to pay for it," said Mouse, who had her own money for the trip.

"That's sweet of you, Mousie."

"It's the least I can do after single-handedly ruining his trip."

"He's probably better off flying home where his family can take care of him."

"I don't think so," said Mouse. "I think he wanted to see the country."

Suzanne was silent for a long moment. "Well, he wouldn't like driving with us and stopping at all the tourist attractions."

"I don't see why not."

"Mouse, did you invite him along with us?"

"We talked about it."

"And?"

"I think he should come with us, Mom. I think he needs looking after."

"If he needs looking after, they shouldn't have released him from the hospital."

"I think that was probably his idea, and now he's regretting it. What if he falls, Mom? What if he falls and he's all alone?"

"We can't just invite a strange man along with us."

"Oh, Mom, you talk as though he could be dangerous. We're talking about Billy. I think he's really nice."

"I'll think about it."

"That always means no."

"Look, while you're out with Daryl tonight, I'll talk it over with Billy. But I can't see that bouncing around in our car is going to be good for him."

"I thought about that," said Mouse. "I think he needs a couple of pillows. He can put them under his leg and cushion the shock."

"We could all use that," said Suzanne.

BILLY DIDN'T KNOW WHY he was watching a soap opera.

Part of the reason was that Mouse had asked him to and part of the reason was that the pain was too bad to sleep and there was nothing to do in the room but watch television and nothing on the TV except soap operas. But it sure was boring watching people sitting around and talking just like in real life except that these people didn't do anything else but talk. Real people finally stopped talking and got up and did something.

Billy thought of getting up and going out and sitting by the pool. He couldn't go in the pool. He couldn't get his leg wet yet, which meant sponge baths for the duration, something that never made him feel quite clean.

He had looked out the window to check out who was sitting by the pool, but all he saw were some rowdy children having a war with the water. He didn't ordinarily mind rowdy children but they were the kind who would run around the pool and slip and fall, and what they fell on just might be his leg. It looked too dangerous to go out there.

But if these two bitchy women didn't stop talking he was going to make the effort to get up off the bed and at least turn the sound down so he didn't have to hear what they were saying. Bitch, bitch, bitch, that's all they did, and mostly about men. And you got the feeling, even while they were bitching about the man, that they both wanted the man but didn't want the other one to know it.

He heard one of the women say, "Well, I for one will be glad to see the last of Barbara Jean," and Billy's ears suddenly pricked up. Had she really said Barbara Jean?

The other woman said, "She wouldn't be leaving if you hadn't made her life a living hell."

"It wasn't hard to do," said the other. "Barbara Jean just seems to thrive on unhappiness. Actually, I figure I'm doing her a favor."

What was this with Barbara Jean? First in the restaurant, now on the TV screen. He had gone his whole life without ever hearing the name Barbara Jean, and now it seemed to be assuming epidemic proportions.

And then one of them said, "Watch out," and onto the screen came Barbara Jean, or rather Suzanne, but he hardly recognized her because she had such a sweet sorrowful look on her face and she was wearing a dress and low-heeled shoes. Her dress had a high neck in contrast to the bitches who wore tight, low-cut dresses and high-heeled shoes. And her dress was pink, while their dresses were black and red, respectively.

He guessed it all had to be spelled out for the audience. He didn't know why. He could have figured out the good guys and the bad guys just by what they said.

Barbara Jean said, "Am I interrupting anything?" and Billy wouldn't have recognized the voice, either, if he hadn't heard that sudden change in Suzanne's voice in the restaurant. It was a sweet voice, but it had a slight bit of whine to it that wasn't appealing.

The lesser of the bitches said to Barbara Jean, "We hear you're leaving town."

Barbara Jean, her hands folded in front of her, dropped her eyes. "I think it's for the best."

The other woman, the one who was the bitchier of the two, said, "Vic really dumped on you, didn't he?"

Now tears could be seen in Barbara Jean's eyes. In a whispery, whiny little voice she said, "I don't think he meant to."

The other two women could barely contain their smiles. Billy found himself actually waiting to hear what would come next, but what came next was a commercial for floor wax, and Suzanne or no Suzanne, he got up off the bed and hopped over to the TV and turned it off.

Well, it was a living, he guessed, and no doubt a well paid one, but it sure seemed a shame to see a lively, articulate woman like Suzanne playing a mealymouthed, cowardly woman like Barbara Jean. Hell, he would have cast her as one of the bitches. Whoever cast her in that part didn't have any smarts as far as Billy could make out.

But at least it solved the mystery.

Chapter Four

Mouse went off at six with Daryl and, shortly after that, Suzanne was on the phone to a friend of hers from Yorktown Towers in New York when she heard a thumping sound coming from the wall behind her bed, which meant it was coming from Billy's room. She didn't think he was signaling her as there were phones in the rooms he could have used. If he was in trouble he surely would have yelled.

Suzanne said to Abbie. "The cowboy I was telling you about is banging on the wall."

"He probably wants you to join him," said Abbie.

"For what? I told you, his leg is bad."

"That wouldn't stop a lot of guys."

"He seems pretty nice."

"Then why don't you drive him home? Hell, Suzanne, you wanted some adventure. Now it's dropped into your lap and you act like you're not going to take advantage of it."

"I wanted adventure, which didn't mean meeting a man."

"Oh, come on, Suzanne, this is Abbie you're talking to. Since when does adventure not include a man?" Suzanne had to hand it to her friend. She had recently broken off a four-year relationship but she kept her perspective, kept hoping. "And he's a cowboy to boot. I mean, how perfect can you get?"

"The timing's not right. I'm driving Mouse to college."

"And Mouse is out on a date and you're sitting in a motel room calling me instead of getting to know a real, live cowboy."

Abbie always did hand out such wise advice. Probably all that practice at being an assistant D.A.

There was another thump and Suzanne began to worry. "I think I better go see what happened to him."

"Wear something pretty."

"Will you quit it, Abbie?"

"All right, don't wear something pretty. But call me and let me know what happens, okay?"

"Say hello to Marielle for me," said Suzanne. She'd heard Jaime was still down in Victory House in New Orleans. Only Abbie and Marielle were left in Yorktown Towers.

The thumping continued after she hung up. She went next door and knocked at his door. "Are you all right in there?" she called through the door.

The thumping sound stopped and there was silence. After a moment she heard, "Come on in, it's not locked."

Suzanne opened the door and saw Billy, one boot off and one boot on, his shod foot up against the wall with the top of his boot hooked on the corner of his headboard. She surmised this explained the thumping.

"I suppose there's a reason for that," said Suzanne, moving into the room and letting the door close behind her.

"I can't get the damn thing off," said Billy, sounding frustrated. "Not only can't I get it off without my thing-amajig, but I think my foot's swollen and now my knee's killing me from trying to get this damn boot off."

Suzanne moved over to his bed and unhooked the boot from the headboard. Being careful, she tried pulling gently on the boot with both hands. "Thingamajig?"

"Some long thing with a thing on the end they give patients to get their shoes off and on. And to pick up stuff from the floor. Now it looks like I'm going to die with my boots on." He sounded like a kid. He sounded very much like Mouse had sounded at age four when she couldn't quite get the hang of tying her own shoes.

Suzanne began to tug a little harder but nothing was happening except that Billy was getting a pained expression on his face and she was afraid she was hurting him. He wasn't moaning. She had a feeling he wouldn't moan in front of a woman. But she knew if he were all alone he'd be doing a hell of a lot more than moaning.

"Are you supposed to be wearing tight boots like this?" Suzanne asked him.

"They're not usually tight," said Billy. "These boots are well worn in; I think my foot got larger."

"I think running shoes would be a lot more comfortable for you."

"I don't want to look like some asinine New Yorker," said Billy. "If I wore running shoes where I come from they'd laugh me out of the state."

Suzanne considered taking off one of her running shoes and smacking him across the mouth with it. She controlled herself and gave him a sweet, phony, Barbara Jean smile as she gave one final tug on his boot.

Billy did moan this time, although it sounded more like a cry of pain. Suzanne gently placed his boot—with the foot in it—on the bed. "I think you're going to have to get it cut off."

Billy was looking very pale, and sweat had broken out on his forehead. "At least you didn't say 'we.' "

"Why would I say we?"

"That's what the nurse would've said. She would've said *we* were going to have *our* boot cut off. They treat you like children in hospitals, take all your dignity away."

Suzanne pulled up a chair beside his bed and sat down. He looked bad. He certainly didn't look as though he should be out of the hospital. "Billy, did you call your family?"

He nodded.

"I think the best thing would be to put you on a plane, get you home and let your mother take care of you."

"My mother?"

"You have a mother, don't you?"

"Mom isn't about to take care of me. She works."

Somehow that didn't fit the image Suzanne had of Billy's mother. She had pictured women in Wyoming as quintessential earth mothers, not working women. She pictured Billy's mother as a plump woman with her hair in a bun and wearing a red-checked apron as she stirred a pot of soup over a black iron stove. Or maybe a gaunt woman, half Indian, who broke horses bareback and carried a bullwhip at all times. And it just might be Suzanne had seen too many Westerns as a kid.

"Maybe your parents could get in a practical nurse for you."

"I don't need a nurse; I can take care of myself."

"You can't even get your boot off."

"I got it off last night. And if that thingamajig hadn't gone over the cliff with the car, I'd be able to get it off tonight."

"If you're trying to make me feel guilty, it's not going to work."

Billy managed a grin. "I guess I'll have to think of something else."

"Is your family wiring you some money?"

"Nope. The problem is, you need ID to pick up the money from Western Union, and I don't have any ID."

"They're just going to leave you here? Destitute?"

"I was going to throw myself on your mercy, Barbara Jean."

"You can knock off the Barbara Jean."

"I happened to watch a little bit of *Reach for the Sky* today. You sure are sweet on that show. Just the kind of woman a man would like to throw over his shoulder and take home to his folks."

Suzanne had a feeling she had Mouse to thank for that. "Well, I'm not getting paid to be sweet now, and I doubt you're in condition to even throw a crutch over your shoulder."

"I didn't mean me. I try not to be that overtly macho; I leave that to my twin."

"You mean there're two of you?"

"Not exactly. Not if you mean do I have a double on the ranch. My twin is a woman. She's the one I called. Wendy's sending me some money and a credit card by express mail. It ought to be here in the morning."

"They have express mail in Wyoming?"

"Sure we do. Course it's not as fast as pony express, but we make do."

"What about tonight? I thought I'd take you shopping but you don't look like you're up to it."

"I could sure use a change of clothes. But if it's a choice between a change of clothes and getting up off this bed in the near future, I guess I'll go with the ones I'm wearing.''

"If you want, you could write me down your sizes and what you need, and if I get everything wrong, we can always return them in the morning."

"Couple of T-shirts, some skivvies and another pair of Levi's would do me. And some socks."

"Could I make a suggestion, Billy?"

Billy just waited in silence.

"I know you think we New Yorkers dress strange, but wouldn't shorts and sneakers be more comfortable? I mean, I doubt whether you'll be riding the range anytime in the near future."

"Next you'll be trying to get my Stetson off my head. And speaking of hats, is there some reason for that charming one of the baseball variety you're wearing on your head?"

Suzanne took her sunglasses out of her pocket and put them on. "It's a disguise; do you recognize me?"

"Are you disguising Suzanne or are you disguising Barbara Jean?"

"Barbara Jean."

"Well, I only saw her briefly today, but I'd say Barbara Jean probably wouldn't be wearing a baseball hat. I picture Barbara Jean as more the type to be wearing some pink hat with little flowers on it."

Suzanne reached over and grabbed his cowboy hat off his head. He tried to take it away from her, didn't succeed, then sat there looking as though he felt naked without it. She took a good look at him, decided he looked even younger without it and handed it back to him. "Just wanted to see you without your disguise," she said.

"This isn't a disguise."

"It's not exactly what people wear when they go to New York, either. I'll bet they got a charge out of you in the hospital."

Billy didn't say anything.

"Did they get that off of you when you were on the operating table?"

Billy ignored her.

Suzanne put on her Barbara Jean smile and her Barbara Jean voice and said, "Why, honey, I'm just trying to cheer you up. Don't cowboys have a sense of humor?"

Billy started to grin. "Go back to your New York voice before I start to throw up."

Suzanne got up, said, "That's more like it; I'll be back in a minute," and headed out of the room. She had remembered the ice machine around the corner of the building. Maybe if they could get the swelling down, the boot would come off.

"COLORADO? WHY COLORADO?"

They were sitting in a bar out on the highway, Daryl drinking a beer and Mouse drinking Perrier, something that had made Daryl snort when she had ordered it. The place was filled mostly with young people, and Daryl had told her a live group played there on weekends. Mouse hadn't been in a bar before on a date, probably because the boys she dated in New York weren't old enough. It made her feel very adult and she didn't even mind that she had to drink Perrier because even that seemed adult, much more so than to just order a beer. Beer was something you sneaked drinks of in high school, not something you ordered as an adult.

"I like to ski," Mouse told him.

"Ski? I thought you were from New York City?"

"It's possible to live in New York and still ski," said Mouse. "I go to Vermont to ski."

"I don't get it. Are you going there for an education or to ski?"

"To ski."

"Correct me if I'm wrong, Mouse, but isn't that a lot of money to spend just to ski?"

"Well, I'll probably be educated in the process. I'm pretty tired of school, though. If it weren't for the skiing, I would've put up an argument about going to college. I'm really sick of school, Daryl; I'm ready to start living my life."

Mouse looked around and saw that she was getting a lot of attention. It wasn't just from the guys, either, although their attention was more blatant. She wasn't sure whether it was the result of her black leather miniskirt and black leather bra, the bra worn beneath an open silk shirt—hadn't any of them ever heard of Madonna?—or whether it was the green streaks she had sprayed into her hair. At any rate, the other young people were an unimaginatively dressed bunch, most of them in shorts and T-shirts.

"Half the town knows who you are already," said Daryl, "and the other half will know by morning."

"You mean because of my mother?"

"Your mother? What's she got to do with it?"

Mouse decided not to say anything about her mother as Barbara Jean. Her friends in New York had all found it strange that her mother was in a soap opera, as though that showed a real lack of taste and ambition.

"What're you talking about, Daryl?"

"About your knocking that car off the cliff. That's the most exciting thing that's happened here all summer."

"This must really be a boring town. If that happened in New York, it wouldn't even get mentioned in the papers."

"It's not the Big Apple, that's for sure."

"It's not even close."

"Hell, no," said Daryl. "Why, I imagine you could walk all over town by yourself, any hour of the day or the night, and no one would even dream of mugging you. No one even has that kind of imagination."

"I was never mugged in New York."

"Tell me something, Mouse. How many locks did you have on your door in New York?"

"One."

Daryl looked doubtful. "Judging by what I see on TV, people in New York had several locks on their doors."

"We don't need several locks; our building has a doorman and a good security system."

"Okay, that's the difference. No one here has a doorman *or* a security system, and no one ever has to lock their door."

"Nothing gets stolen?"

"If it does, it's usually done by a little kid and whatever was taken gets returned."

"Well, all I can say, Daryl, is you must have the world's most boring job. Why would anyone want to be a cop in a town with no crime?"

"We're traffic more than anything else. Accidents on the interstate, things like that."

"And that satisfies you? Your ambition in life is to officiate at traffic accidents?"

"Well, when you compare it to skiing, I guess it doesn't sound all that exciting."

"Skiing *is* exciting."

"Come on," said Daryl, standing up and holding out his hand to her. "That's my song playing on the juke-box. Let's give all these folks a good view of you."

BILLY FELT LIKE A FREAK. He'd had a beautiful woman in his room and there he was, dirty, sweaty, one smelly foot out of a boot and the other stuck inside, lying on his bed as helpless as a baby, near tears of frustration because he couldn't seem to do anything right. He wasn't even sure he was going to be able to get his damn pants off by himself.

He took off his Stetson and threw it across the room. What he'd like would be a shower and then a couple of beers. Only he wasn't allowed a shower until the stitches came out and he wasn't allowed alcohol with the pain pills he was taking. And if he couldn't have either of those, then he'd like Suzanne under the covers with him, only there wasn't a whole lot of point to that, either, because he had to stay on his back and he couldn't risk hurting his leg. Except part of him didn't know all that because part of him had been straining to stand at attention the entire time she had been there.

The crazy thing was, he hadn't had that kind of itch in the hospital, and some of the nurses had been real pretty. He had an itch for Suzanne, though, and he only hoped she hadn't been aware of it. Embarrassing enough just not being able to do anything about it.

He grabbed an extra pillow and shoved it behind his head and picked up the Stephen King book Mouse had brought him. Maybe he could scare the feeling away.

He hadn't gone more than three pages when there was a knock on the door, quickly followed by the door opening and Suzanne walking in.

"I brought you some ice," she said, "to get the swelling down," and he had an idea where that ice would do the most good, but he didn't say anything. He just watched her as she got a towel out of his bathroom, dumped the contents of the ice bucket in it, then approached the bed.

"I don't know how much good this is going to do," she said. "I'm not even sure it'll work with your boot on."

She placed the ice-filled towel over his foot. "Just leave it there until I get back."

"You're leaving?"

"I thought I'd get us some dinner. I don't feel like going back to that restaurant again, but there's a Burger King nearby. That okay with you?"

"That'd be great."

"And if you tell me what size shoes you wear, I'll get you something you can slip in and out of easier."

"You can forget the shoes," said Billy.

"Then I'll just take this with me," said Suzanne, picking up the boot that was on the floor and walking out the door with it.

He felt like throwing the book after her, but then he'd be left with nothing to do, so instead he just muttered, "Damn bossy woman," to the closed door. Only she wasn't all that bossy; she was just trying to be helpful. He knew bossy women; he had grown up with bossy women; and she wasn't even a contender.

MOUSE HAD DONE A LOT of dancing in her eighteen years but most of it had been with other girls and all of it had been to fast music. So she was pretty surprised when a slow record came on and Daryl put his arms around her and pulled her close—very close—and started to nuzzle his nose in her hair. She was pretty surprised because she found she liked it and she wondered why none of the boys she had dated in high school had ever danced with her like this.

Probably because she would have punched them out, she decided, pulling a little bit away from Daryl and giving him a suspicious look. Did he think he could get away with this because she was a tourist from New York?

"What's the problem?" asked Daryl, trying to pull her close to him again.

"Aren't we dancing a little close?"

"This? Are you serious? Take a look around you."

Mouse glanced around the dance floor and saw that all the couples were dancing just as close. Some even closer, if that was possible. Most of the guys had their hands on the girls' bottoms and some of the girls were doing the same. A lot of them were kissing. At that point she began to feel like a voyeur and stopped watching. She didn't pull away again when Daryl pulled her close, though.

Michael Jackson was singing and she thought Michael Jackson was a real weirdo, but the song was nice and even though it was slow it had a good, steady beat to it, and she suddenly realized the reason she was aware of the beat was that Daryl was gently moving against her in time to the music and it really felt good.

She was pretty sure that anything that felt that good must be bad, but she found she didn't care. She was eighteen, she was an adult, and if she wanted to be bad she'd be bad. Anyway, how bad could it be if it could be done on a dance floor in a crowd of people?

She began to move against him a little in return and found that felt even better. It also seemed to be raising the temperature of the room by a good few degrees.

And speaking of degrees, Daryl's hands were beginning to inch down her back a little bit at a time, slowly moving in the direction of her little bitty miniskirt. Her skirt was so short she had friends whose mothers wouldn't let them wear ones like it. Her mother couldn't say anything, though, because her mother also wore them. She also knew for a fact that her mother also wore little, tiny bikini panties under them, just like Mouse did. Her mother didn't have any as tiny as the ones she was wearing tonight, though. These consisted of an infinitesimal scrap of black lace and a T-shaped piece of elastic. She felt naked underneath her skirt. And at the moment, that felt terrific.

Daryl's hands had apparently reached their goal and were now pausing, waiting for some reaction from her. They were cupping her rear end and, no doubt, pulling her skirt up even higher. She thought of shrugging those hands away. She knew if she tried he'd give it up and put his hands back where they were before, but she didn't want to shrug them away. She very much wanted to see what he'd do next.

She felt his lips on her neck, which momentarily diverted her, but not to where she couldn't feel his hands grasping onto her and pulling her in even closer. And now all the moving against each other was doing even more to shake her composure, which was already almost nonexistent.

Daryl left one hand where it was and brought the other one up to raise her chin. For a moment they looked into each other's eyes, and then his mouth closed over hers and his was forcing hers open, and then she felt his tongue begin to play with her teeth until she opened them up and let his tongue in, and then, with dizzying speed, she was caught up in the most passionate kiss she had ever imagined. And then the hand that had lifted her chin was moving down between their bodies, brushing over her leather bra and practically short-circuiting her nervous system. She was absolutely stunned and couldn't imagine why he was suddenly breaking off the kiss and dropping his hands, and then she realized that the song was over and the next song coming on was a fast one.

"I could use a drink," said Daryl, taking hold of her hand and leading her back to the table.

Mouse felt she could use a lot more than a drink. Was this love she was feeling? Was this love or had she missed out on a lot when she had opted to remain a virgin in high school? Not that her options had been great, but she was sure that one of the boys she had dated might have known something about sex.

"Aren't we going to dance anymore?" Mouse asked him.

His smile was knowing. "Oh, hell, yes, we're going to dance some more."

Mouse gave a sigh of pure enjoyment.

SHE WAS BACK in about forty minutes and by that time Billy actually was getting scared. This King book was something else, playing on every fear known to man. He almost jumped when he heard the door open, so sure he was that the bogeyman was about to come in and get him. Hell, he hadn't even *thought* about the bogeyman since he was about eight years old, but the guy sure could write to inspire terror.

Suzanne put down some bags and approached the bed. He didn't know whether the ice had managed to get the swelling down, but it had sure managed to melt fast and soak his bed clean through. It was a good thing the room had two beds or he would be forced to sleep on wet sheets all night.

She grabbed hold of his boot and tried pulling on it again. It caught for a moment, but then he could feel it giving way and in a few moments she had the boot off and was removing his sock.

"I don't know how you got that on this morning," she said, looking down at his swollen foot.

"It wasn't swollen this morning."

"Let's get those pants off, too."

Right. Just what he wanted, having her see him with his pants off.

She moved around to the side of the bed and started unstrapping his leg brace. "Does this have to stay on all night?"

"No. Just when I'm walking."

The leg brace came off, and then she made a tentative move toward his belt before thinking better of it. She went over to one of the bags and pulled out a pair of khaki shorts. "I thought you might be more comfortable in these."

Of course he'd feel more comfortable in them. Skintight Levi's were fine for maybe eight hours a day, but after that his stomach felt a need to breathe. "Where'd those come from?"

"They're mine."

"I'm not wearing women's clothes."

"They're unisex," said Suzanne. "Actually, they're probably not even that—I bought them in a men's store."

"I'll wear them tonight, but I'm not wearing them out in public."

"Suit yourself," said Suzanne.

Billy undid his belt, unzipped his fly, then pulled the bedspread over to cover his crotch. "Maybe you could try pulling my pants off. Gently."

Suzanne took hold of the bottoms of his pants. "Can you lift your rear up a little?"

Billy obliged, then watched as his pants were removed. It felt real good to have them off.

She was looking at his leg. "Does the Ace bandage have to stay on?"

"It protects the dressings, which I've got to change."

"You need some help with that?"

"Nah, I can manage. I don't do it until I go to bed."

Suzanne put his feet through the pair of shorts and drew them up to his knees. She then turned her back while he took over. They felt good, a hell of a lot better than the jeans had felt.

"I can't wait to see the shoes," he said.

"They're not really running shoes," she told him, "they're just cheap imitations, but good enough for the amount of walking you're going to be doing. The really good thing about them is they fasten with Velcro, which makes them easy to get on and off. I thought of just getting you some rubber thongs, but I was afraid you might trip and fall."

"I could get them on if I could reach them," said Billy.

"You can't reach your feet?"

"Not the left one. Not without the thingamajig."

"Do you think you can get yourself over to the table to eat?"

"Course I can get myself over. I'm not a cripple. Well, maybe I am, but you're acting as though I didn't get this far on my own."

Instead of fussing or trying to help him over, she just shrugged and carried the food over to the table. He was glad of that. A little help was okay, but he didn't want her to start mothering him. Because if she started mothering him then she'd start thinking of him as a kid, and he sure as hell didn't want her thinking that. Putting him on the same level as Mouse would be the kiss of death to anything romantic developing between them.

Oh, hell, who was he kidding? The chance of anything romantic developing between them was about as great as the chance of the bogeyman walking in.

Suzanne had envisioned enjoying her nights on the road with Mouse. She thought they could find interesting places to eat, see a few movies, do some serious talking; it would be a long time before they got the opportunity to talk again.

What she hadn't envisioned was Mouse going out on a date and leaving her with nothing to do but watch television in her room. Of course this would be the exception rather than the norm unless Mouse got in car accidents in every town they stopped in and thus continued to meet young policemen.

Not that she hadn't had Billy for company, and Billy had been fine until shortly after they had finished eating, when she saw that Billy was having a hard time keeping his eyes open even though she had been her most entertaining, regaling him with stories of disasters that had happened on *Reach for the Sky*.

When not only his eyes were closed, but his mouth had dropped open and she knew that no story, no matter how amusing, was going to revive him, she gathered all the trash from their meal together, dumped it in the wastebasket and returned to her room.

She turned on the TV, found that all three channels were carrying the same ball game and turned it back off. She lay down on the bed with one of the books she had brought with her. The books had been chosen not for entertainment, but for knowledge, and she found that while an entertaining book could keep her awake, a treatise on the underlying problems in the Middle East didn't quite do the trick, and pretty soon her own eyes were closing and she finally quit fighting it and relaxed completely.

MOUSE AND DARYL were squeezed together in the passenger side of his pickup. More specifically, Mouse was on his lap and their lips were glued together and even though it had cooled off somewhat when the sun went down, the humidity was on the rise and a thunderstorm seemed imminent and Mouse's leather skirt and bra were plastered to her skin with sweat. All of which might have been uncomfortable in other circumstances, but Mouse wasn't complaining. Mouse was feeling the kinds of stirrings that high-school boys had never evoked in her. In fact, they were more than stirrings at this point; they were more like thunderbolts.

He came up for air for a moment and looked deeply into her eyes and Mouse shifted a little, bringing her chest more directly in contact with his chest and sighing in the process.

"It's getting late," said Daryl, not sounding overly worried about the fact.

"I don't care."

"I don't want your mother calling the police, reporting you missing."

"Why would she call the police? You're the police."

"It's been known to happen," said Daryl, shifting his legs and making his lap even more comfortable for her.

Mouse didn't want to go home because that would mean the night was over and she'd never see Daryl again. Why did she have to meet someone like him on the road? Why not in New York, or at least when she got to college? Why now, when nothing could ever come of it? He was perfect for her. Not only did she love his looks, but she loved his quick mind and sense of humor.

As though sensing her thoughts, Daryl said, "I don't think I'm going to let you leave."

"You don't see me trying to leave."

"I mean tomorrow. I don't think I want you to just walk out of my life like that."

She burrowed her head between his shoulder and chin and moved her cheek against his neck. "There's no way Mom's going to spend another night here."

"Maybe I'll lock you up in jail. Reckless driving, endangering the lives of others. I should be able to come up with something."

"Will you visit me in jail?"

"Hell, I'll lock myself in there with you."

Mouse felt an almost painful surge of desire at the thought. She rubbed her breasts against his chest and heard his sharp intake of breath. In a moment one hand was forcing itself between their chests and she moved back a little to give him room to maneuver. His hand went to one leather-clad breast and squeezed and Mouse felt a tremor go from her breast straight down, and she could feel an involuntary parting of her legs.

"Oh, God, you're the sexiest girl I've ever seen," murmured Daryl, his hand trying to move inside her bra but not finding any space.

Mouse had never thought of herself as sexy and loved the idea. In a move she never would have pictured herself making, she reached for the clasp on the front of the bra and undid it in one quick motion. It was maybe the most daring move she had ever made in her life.

Daryl was equally daring. He was pulling her up on his lap so that his mouth was in line with her breasts, and

then he was sucking on one of her nipples and she was
clasping her arms around his neck and pulling his head
in harder and harder, trying to bury her breast in his
mouth.

Daryl's hand was moving up her leg and she spread
them wider, but the skirt was short and tight and she
couldn't get them very far apart without shoving her skirt
clear up to her waist, which seemed a little bit like asking for it, because, while she was quite prepared to ex-
periment like mad, she wasn't quite ready to go all the
way on a first date. Except maybe it was going to be the
last date, and maybe she wasn't going to be able to stop
herself.

Daryl's hand was on her thigh and now his fingers were
crawling inside of the patch of black lace. She felt small
convulsions starting down there that she hoped would
somehow never stop because she had never been so
thrilled over anything in her life and she was wishing she
had experimented a little more in high school, even
though the boys had been jerks, because this was a whole
lot more fun than going to the movies or sitting around
in bars or even dancing as close as she and Daryl had
been dancing most of the evening.

The door to her motel room opened and the light
spilled out, illuminating the truck, and Daryl, thinking
fast, pushed her down out of view. Mouse was soaring
and Daryl's interruption of that flight came as a shock
and a disappointment and a very big loss.

''That's your mom,'' whispered Daryl, peering up over
the dashboard for a look. ''She's going into the next
room.''

''The cowboy's room,'' murmured Mouse.

''Yeah? Those two got something going?''

"I doubt it," said Mouse. "Mom isn't interested in sex." But as soon as she said it she started to question that long-held belief of hers. How could her mother possibly have done with her father what she and Daryl were doing and not be interested in sex? She knew for a fact that she personally would never again not be interested in sex.

Daryl said. "I think maybe you better go in."

"I don't want to go in." But even while she was saying it, she was trying to fasten her bra together, but for some reason her breasts seemed bigger and it was a lot more difficult than usual.

Daryl's hand slid out of her panties and rested for a moment on her thigh. "Stay here with me, Mouse."

"Okay," said Mouse, taking his hand and putting it under her skirt again.

"I don't mean just tonight. I mean stay here. Move in with me."

"Daryl, I can't; I'm going to college."

"Go to college in Cleveland if you have to go to college."

"It's not that easy. I haven't been accepted there."

"I don't want to lose you, Mouse. I've never met anyone like you."

"Well, all you have to do is go to New York. There's all kinds of girls like me there."

"I don't believe it. I don't think I'll find anyone else as perfect for me."

Mouse wasn't at all sure she'd find anyone as perfect as Daryl, but she knew for sure that her mother wasn't going to let her forget about Colorado after the tuition was already paid.

"Couldn't you come visit me? I could put you up in my dorm."

"By then you'll have every guy in the school after you."

"We can talk on the phone; we can write letters."

"You really think writing letters is going to be the same?"

"Couldn't you take some time off and come visit me?"

"I think I love you, Mouse."

"I think I love you, too. I also think I better get in there and wash up a little before Mom gets back."

"I'm never going to see you again, am I?"

"Come have breakfast with us in the morning, Daryl. I'll meet you at that restaurant in town."

"It's going to be worse seeing you for the last time with people around."

"It won't be the last time, Daryl. I'll call you every night, I promise."

"I bet you'll have forgotten me by the time you get to Chicago."

"Don't talk, Daryl, just kiss me again. I want to be able to remember every night what it was like to kiss you. I want to be able to fantasize about it."

Mouse was already seeing herself as a tragic figure, rather like Juliet, when Daryl's mouth once more covered her own.

WHEN SUZANNE WOKE UP she thought she had only dozed for a few minutes. A look at her watch, however, told her it was one-thirty in the morning. She wondered why Mouse's return hadn't awakened her. She looked over at the other bed, surprised that Mouse hadn't turned the lights off, but the other bed was still made up and piled high with Mouse's belongings.

She got up. She was still in that twilight zone of half-remembered dreams and fuzzy thinking and she automatically began to clear off Mouse's bed and turn it down so that she could slip under the covers unhampered when she returned. She had gone that far and was digging in her own bag to find the long, soft T-shirt she slept in when it occurred to her that one-thirty was too late for Mouse to be out with a strange man in a strange town and it was unlike Mouse not to at least call her and tell her she was going to be late. It was something Mouse would have done at home. Neither of them was a paranoid New Yorker, but neither were they unaware of the dangers in the city, and Mouse would never have intentionally caused her mother worry.

She heard a crash from the next room, from Billy's room, and stood still for a moment listening for more. There was only silence and that was more worrisome than the crash. And why was she worrying about Billy? She had enough to worry about with Mouse, she didn't need another person to worry about. But Mouse had no doubt just forgotten the time and Billy might have fallen and hurt himself.

She left the room and went next door, knocking at the door and then opening it and looking in. Billy, looking wild-eyed, was sitting on the end of the bed, his crutches just out of reach on the floor.

"Are you okay?" asked Suzanne.

"I knocked over my crutches and I can't get to them."

Suzanne entered the room and picked up the crutches, handing them to him.

He took them with a hand that was visibly trembling. "I hate it," he said, his eyes on the floor. "I couldn't even reach them."

"You should probably still be in the hospital."

"Do you know how they treat you in the hospital? Like a child. Like some helpless little kid who can't do anything for himself. If I had stayed in there one more day I would've been screaming at the walls.'' He paused for a moment and a slight smile turned up the corners of his mouth. ''Just like I was ready to do in here. I was about ready to scream at the walls because I couldn't do something as simple as pick up my damn crutches and make it to the bathroom.''

''Now you know how it feels to be an actor.''

''An actor? What in hell has this to do with acting?''

Suzanne sat down on the edge of the other bed. ''You get treated like little kids. Like you can't figure out anything for yourself and have to wait for the director to tell you what is so. It's like being a little kid again with your parents making all your decisions for you.''

''Yeah, but there's a major difference. You were getting paid for it. If I was being paid good money to stay in a hospital for a while, maybe it wouldn't have been so bad.''

''It would've been as bad. Actors don't have the pain you've been going through, but other than that it's just as bad. Particularly if you're an actor on the soaps. You get about as much respect as a scab football player who crosses the picket lines.''

Billy set the crutches in front of him and began to slowly lift himself from the bed. She felt an urge to help him but knew that would only add to his feeling of helplessness. Instead, in order to take his mind off his own troubles and because it really was beginning to worry her, she said, ''Mouse isn't home yet; I'm starting to get worried.''

He paused in his slow walk to the bathroom. ''What time is it?''

''Getting close to two.''

''How late is she allowed to stay out?''

"I don't have a curfew for her; I rely on her judgment."

"They why stop relying now?"

She shouldn't have expected him to see her point of view. He would naturally relate to Daryl, to a young man wanting to keep his date out all night if possible. After all, the longer you keep her with you, the more possibility that you'll end up getting everything you want from her.

Billy continued to the bathroom and finally made it. He closed the door and then she didn't hear anything until the flush of the toilet. When he emerged, he asked her, "That stuff you got me at the pharmacy, could you set it out on the bedside table for me?"

Suzanne got the antiseptic and dressings and tape and brought them over to the table. She also pulled back the bedspread on the other bed as the one he had been in still hadn't completely dried.

"Why don't you let me do that for you? Unless it makes you feel helpless."

He sat down on the edge of the bed and carefully placed his crutches between the table and the bed so that they wouldn't fall over. He pulled his left leg up onto the bed and began to unwrap the Ace bandage.

Suzanne didn't know what she had been expecting when the dressing was off but it wasn't such a large, nasty-looking incision with a bloody crust surrounding it.

Billy washed it off with the antiseptic and then opened a dressing and placed it over the knee where the incision still wasn't healing and the scab was split open. He was trying to hold onto the gauze and unroll the tape at the same time and not succeeding.

Suzanne took the tape from his hand and ripped him off a piece. He looked more resigned than grateful when she taped the dressing in place.

"Maybe you're right," said Billy. "Maybe I should get on a plane tomorrow and head for Wyoming."

"How are you going to get up those steep steps to a plane?"

"I don't know. I suppose they have wheelchairs."

Suzanne thought of him being bundled into a wheelchair and treated like a child again. Airline personnel were just as good at that as hospital personnel. She thought of him trying to stretch out his leg in the limited amount of space they provided on a plane; of other passengers trying to climb over him to get to the aisle, perhaps jarring his knee and fouling up his surgery. Not that the Suzuki was going to be that comfortable, but at least he'd have a couple of people along to help him out if he needed it.

Still, she held back suggesting it until he said, "Maybe I should just go back to the hospital."

"They said you could leave, didn't they? I mean, you didn't just walk out without permission, did you?"

"They released me. I think the doctor thought I was going to be back in bed in a few hours, though."

"I'll drive you home, Billy."

"A ride to the airport'll be fine."

"Then why didn't you fly from New York?"

Billy's lower lip was shoved out and she knew the next thing she was going to hear was either a justification or an outright lie. Instead the lip was slowly retracted and he gave her a sheepish grin. "I don't like flying."

"Are you afraid to fly?"

"Let's just say I don't like it much. I'd almost rather walk home from New York than fly."

If that wasn't a fear of flying, she didn't know what it was. "Are you afraid of my driving? I'm a very good driver, really, and I'll only let Mouse drive on open stretches just to give her some practice."

"I'd just be a bother to you."

"Listen, if my daughter's going to start dating on the road, it'll be nice to have some company."

"What the hell, I don't know why I'm giving you an argument about it. I'd be damn grateful for a ride. And for the company."

"Good. Let's get you in bed, then—"

"Don't start coming on like a mother, Barbara Jean."

Suzanne folded her arms across her chest and looked down at him. "All right, put yourself in bed. I'll see you in the morning."

MOUSE WAS IN THEIR ROOM when Suzanne got back.

"Where've you been, Mom?" she asked, her voice sweetly innocent.

"Where have *I* been? I woke up at one-thirty and you weren't home yet."

Mouse shrugged.

"Didn't you think I might worry about you?"

"I'm eighteen now, Mom."

"What's age got to do with it?"

"If I stay out all night in Colorado you won't even know the difference."

"That's right, and if I don't know about it I won't worry, but tonight I knew about it."

"I had a good time, Mom. We went to this place where there was music and dancing and a lot of his friends were there. He's really nice, Mom."

Suzanne was relieved Mouse was home and too tired to discuss it. Anyway, Mouse was right. She'd be able to do whatever she wanted at college and if Suzanne didn't trust her to use her head by this time, it was too late to worry about it.

"What did you do, Mom? Did you and Billy go out somewhere?"

"Billy's in no condition to go out anywhere."

"I really like Billy."

"Good, because he's going with us."

"We're driving him home?"

"I'll probably drop you at college and then take him home."

Mouse got a silly smirk on her face. "You interested in him?"

"Interested?"

"Yeah, you know, like do you have the hots for him?"

"Mouse," Suzanne warned.

"It's perfectly normal, Mom."

"He's not much older than you, Mouse."

"He's thirty-six."

"Did he tell you that?"

Mouse nodded.

"Well, I don't have the hots for him; I just feel sorry for him. Actually, I thought maybe you were developing a crush on him."

"Me? No way! He's much too old for me, Mom. And I'm way past the age where I develop a crush. That's for kids."

"I don't know where you get the idea that eighteen is all that old."

"From you. All my life you've been telling me I'd be a woman at eighteen."

"Well, maybe I exaggerated." Right now, in a pink T-shirt and bikinis, with her hair slicked down from a shower, Mouse looked about twelve. Maybe younger.

Much too young and much too innocent to be going off to college on her own.

Of course Suzanne's mother had probably thought the same about her. And then there she was, two years later, with a husband and a baby. And she could remember very well feeling like a woman.

Chapter Five

Billy was feeling like a new man at breakfast. He had taken the plastic wastebasket liner out of the basket in his room and taped it tightly around his knee, enabling him to take his first shower since before the operation. He wasn't wearing the shorts; he refused to wear the shorts in public, but his new T-shirt was clean and the fake running shoes not only felt good on his feet, they were easier to walk in than his boots.

The hardest thing for him to do was shave. It hadn't been all that difficult in the hospital because the nurse had brought him a basin and he had managed it in bed, but to stand up in the bathroom and use both hands to shave while trying to balance himself against the sink was difficult to manage and tiring on his leg. He neglected to shave this morning on purpose. He kind of liked the bristled, bad look it gave him; he could almost imagine Jesse James's jaw looking exactly the same. He also had the notion that a beard might add a few years to his looks. Suzanne was pretty much treating him like a kid; with a beard, all that might change.

Suzanne sneaked a few glances at his unshaven jaw at the breakfast table but it didn't seem to be turning her on. Maybe she just thought he was a slob.

Mouse was more overt. "Growing a beard?" she asked him straightaway.

"Thinking about it," said Billy, looking over the menu and trying to make up his mind between eggs and sausages and pancakes and sausages. He decided on both with some home fries and biscuits on the side. It was kind of nice to have his appetite back. Even nicer not to be faced with hospital food in the morning.

"You look like you slept well," said Suzanne.

"No thanks to that daughter of yours. Book like to kept me awake all night."

Mouse was grinning. "I think that's his scariest one."

There was something about Mouse this morning. Either she was in a particularly good mood or she perked up in the morning. Her mother wasn't one to perk up in the morning. Suzanne was drinking down coffee like someone dying of thirst. Cindi had noticed her, but Cindi wasn't making a fuss. He couldn't figure out whether Cindi was just being polite and giving Barbara Jean some room or whether the baseball hat and shades had thrown her. Personally, he liked them. They gave her a weird look and it was kind of nice seeing someone as gorgeous and self-confident as Suzanne looking somewhat strange. It was endearing.

Billy knew what was up with Mouse as soon as he spotted Daryl walking in the door looking real casual. Because as soon as Daryl walked in, Mouse was also trying to act real casual, but the level of excitement at the table, which had been minus ten before Daryl arrived, was now hovering way up there and it was all coming from Mouse's side of the table.

Daryl ambled over to their table, looking only mildly interested. Mouse was getting some fast color in her cheeks and if her eyes had been any brighter they could've turned off the overhead lights in the restaurant and saved on electricity.

"Mornin', folks," said Daryl, standing to the side of Mouse's chair and looking down at them. "I see you had to taste some of this fine cuisine again before leaving town."

"Good morning," said Suzanne, her eyes still on the menu. Mouse didn't say anything but instead seemed to be holding her breath.

"Pull up a chair and join us," said Billy, and Daryl did so with alacrity.

Without even looking, Billy was aware of some re-shuffling of legs beneath the table and he would've laid odds that Mouse's leg and Daryl's leg were now touching. He looked over to see if Suzanne was aware of any of this, but she appeared to be oblivious to everything but the menu. Which kind of surprised Billy as he hadn't found the menu all that interesting. Maybe she was the type of person who read the small print on cereal boxes. He wondered what it would be like to spend the rest of his life with a woman who read cereal boxes. Well, if she looked as good in the morning as Suzanne, he guessed he could allow her a few eccentricities.

She sure as hell was looking outrageously good this morning. She was wearing a white denim miniskirt that just managed to cover the very tops of her thighs when she was sitting down, and a skimpy navy-blue tank top that was cut low enough on the sides so that if she moved her arms he caught glimpses of the whites of her breasts. He could hardly wait to watch her drive in that top. If he was driving and she was beside him in that top, he'd be quite capable of knocking any number of cars off cliffs. He wasn't so crazy about the thick, white socks that practically fell around her ankles, but he had to admit that the sight of her golden legs coming up out of those white socks was a sight to behold. Every bit as alluring as Venus rising out of that half shell or whatever it was, and he wasn't even a leg man, damn it, but maybe that was a direct result of all the legs he ever saw being encased in jeans. If cowgirls wore minis would there be a revolt on the range?

Did all women in New York dress like this? He wondered if he had walked out of the hospital and away from all those nurses covered up in white, whether he would have seen an entire city of sexy women in skimpy outfits. If so, he blew his chance; it was for damn sure he'd never see anything like that in Wyoming.

The thing about those skirts. The really sexy thing about those skirts was that the women wearing them were right there. Easily accessible. You didn't have to imagine undressing them. All you had to do was imagine that skirt being lifted just half an inch, and there you were. Bingo! And these sure weren't suitable thoughts for the breakfast table, were they? Maybe it was something in those painkillers he was living on. Maybe they had some ingredient that worked on the libido in an inverse ratio to how they worked on the pain.

Now Mouse. Mouse was safer to think about. Mouse was dressed exactly the same as her mother except that Mouse's mini and tank top were pink, which made the top even more revealing than her mother's and he could see that that little fact hadn't escaped Daryl's notice. Hell, it hadn't escaped his notice, and he wasn't turned on by kids. And what the hell was a mother doing letting her teenage daughter dress like that, only if the mother dressed like that he didn't suppose there was much she could say.

Times had sure changed. If Wendy had ever tried to
sneak out of the house in an outfit like that their mother
would have taken a horsewhip to her. And if his mother
had ever looked like Suzanne, well, all he could say was
that his home life might have turned into some Greek
tragedy.

Billy felt a stirring in his groin and made a concerted
effort to get his mind off tank tops and miniskirts and, in
particular, what was under those miniskirts, and tried to
focus instead on what he was going to eat for breakfast,
but in the light of other things, more interesting things,
his appetite for food was rapidly diminishing.

Hot damn! He was having a great time already and the
trip with them hadn't even started.

"I hear you kids had a good time last night," Suzanne was saying to Daryl, and Billy noticed that Daryl's
cheeks were also acquiring a little healthy color and that
legs were once again shifting beneath the table.

"We went dancing," said Daryl, but it sounded half
like a question, as though he was unsure what Mouse had
told her mother.

"That sounds like fun," said Suzanne, but not
sounding particularly interested.

"Your daughter's a good dancer," said Daryl, and
Billy instantly read a double meaning in that and saw
Mouse starting to choke on the drink of water she had
been taking, but Suzanne still wasn't noticing anything
and Billy felt like saying, "Listen, if you spent as much
time watching your daughter as you do reading that
menu, you might learn a thing or two."

It was strange. Really strange. Three fourths of the
occupants at the table seemed to be running in high gear
on an excess of sexual energy, while the fourth occupant

seemed to be totally oblivious of what was going on all around her.

"I almost forgot," Daryl said to Billy, "the people over to the motel said to tell you your express mail arrived."

"My credit cards," said Billy. "Does this place take credit cards?"

"Not that I know of," said Daryl, but now that his duty was done his attention was once more directed to Mouse.

"We'll work something out," said Suzanne, but by that time Billy's eyes were once more peeking into her tank top and admiring the portion of her skin where the tan line stopped and the pearly white began, and it took him all of several seconds before he realized she was talking about money.

MOUSE WAS TRYING to figure out a way she could be alone with Daryl for a minute before they left, but there wasn't a way, or if there was she sure couldn't find it. His leg had been tight up against hers under the table, making her feel so warm and excited it took several glasses of cold water just to calm her down. And because of all that water she decided she better visit the ladies' room before they left, and she was hoping that Daryl would follow her, that maybe they'd get a chance to kiss goodbye in the hall leading off the kitchen, but instead her mother had followed her and that put an end to any thoughts of goodbye kisses or anything else.

She wondered how people with steady sex lives survived. She hadn't even been able to sleep last night. She had gone through so many instant replays in her mind of what had happened between her and Daryl that sleep never did come.

And now here he was beside her and she wanted him to touch her in the worst way but her mother was directly across the table and there wasn't a thing they could do. The rest room hadn't worked. She couldn't even let the others get in the car first and give Daryl a quick kiss goodbye because she couldn't get into the back seat after the others were seated in the front.

She was pretty sure she was in love. And it wasn't just the sex, either, because she loved his thick, sandy-blond hair and his green eyes that narrowed just like a cat's and had a look in them that made her melt, and the way his narrow hips moved in his pants when he walked and the way he said her name so that it sounded almost like a name in a foreign language. And she was crazy about the way he treated her like a woman. It was the first time in her life any guy had treated her like a woman.

Mouse could see that Billy was aware that something was going on between her and Daryl. Hell, anyone with half his eyesight ought to be able to see that. Her mom, of course, wasn't aware of anything. This was partly because her mom still thought of her as a baby and partly because her mom needed reading glasses and refused to wear them so that now she was slowly trying to make out the items on the menu and seeing only a blur instead, but she wasn't about to break down and ask Mouse to read it to her with anyone else around. Which meant her mom was going to have a hard time on the trip whenever they stopped to eat. She'd probably just order a hamburger for most meals, figuring that any menu would have a hamburger on it.

Ninety-nine percent of Mouse was focused on Daryl, but the other one percent was aware of what was going on with Billy. And what was going on with Billy at the moment was that he couldn't seem to take his eyes off her mom. And, of course, her mom was also oblivious of this. After playing Barbara Jean for fifteen years her mom had a totally false image of herself. Because Barbara Jean didn't have any sex appeal, her mom saw herself the same way. But she was wrong. Mouse had been out in public with her mom enough to know that men found her sexy as hell, even though her mother would deny it if Mouse said so.

She guessed maybe she was kind of like her mother. She had never thought of herself as sexy, either, until she had walked into that bar with Daryl last night and saw that half the guys in the place couldn't tear their eyes away from her, but he also couldn't tear his hands away. And when one of his hands disappeared briefly under the table and Mouse felt it come to rest on her thigh, Mouse thought she would die. And not from pleasure, either, because that went without saying. No, what she could die from was knowing they'd be leaving in a few minutes and Daryl wasn't going to be around to touch her again.

"LAST CHANCE if you want me to turn off for Cleveland," said Suzanne, glancing over at Billy. He had the seat pushed back all the way so that his leg had room to fully stretch out, and she had bought a couple of pillows from the motel to cushion his knee, but he nonetheless didn't look all that comfortable. In fact he seemed somewhat agitated and seemed to be watching her arm on the steering wheel. Maybe he was a little gun-shy from having his car demolished by theirs and he was going to keep an eye out in case she made a wrong move. Or maybe he was just one of those people who weren't totally at ease unless they were doing the driving. She was rather like that herself.

"Trying to get rid of me already?" asked Billy.

"Mother, leave him alone. You're fine up there, aren't you, Billy?"

"I'm not trying to get rid of you," said Suzanne. "The way this car bounces along, I just want to make sure your leg's not hurting."

"Makes me feel at home," said Billy. "It's rather like the motion of a horse."

"He's probably not even a cowboy," Suzanne said to Mouse. "He probably dresses like a cowboy to impress the ladies, while actually he sells insurance back home in Wyoming."

"I ought to sell insurance," said Billy. "There's more money in it."

"You going to be able to ride a horse again?" asked Mouse.

"I'll be able to ride," said Billy. "The problem is going to be mounting and dismounting. The horses kind of prefer that you get on and off from their left side, but I doubt I'll be able to put all my weight on my left leg. At least not for a hell of a long time."

Suzanne was glad to hear Mouse participate in the conversation. Mouse had said very little since they started off this morning. She hadn't eaten much breakfast, either, although Billy more than made up for it. While Suzanne had cereal and fruit and Mouse had coffee and Danish, Billy had ordered everything on the breakfast menu and doubles of some items. Suzanne wondered if it was all the riding that kept him skinny or whether he was just trying to make up for all the bad hospital food.

Daryl had come into the restaurant while they were eating breakfast and joined them at their table. She thought it was sweet of him to come in and say goodbye to Mouse. Mouse seemed a little ill at ease while he was there so Suzanne had taken up the slack in the conversation and given Mouse the time to pull herself together. The problem was, Mouse hadn't had much experience with boys. She hadn't gone to the kind of high school Suzanne had gone to where dating and parties took precedence over academic matters.

She wasn't sure Mouse had ever even kissed a boy. Which was kind of sweet in a way, but that would no doubt make her backward socially when she got to college.

Suzanne reached up and took her baseball cap off, letting her hair blow in the wind. She handed it to Billy, but instead of putting it on the floor, he removed his Stetson, handed it back to Mouse and put the baseball cap on his head.

She looked over at him for a moment and there was no longer a cowboy seated next to her. Running shoes, jeans, a T-shirt and a baseball cap had all contrived to change his image from man of the west to Mr. Anywhere U.S.A. It made him look younger, too.

"What're you looking at?" asked Billy.

"You. You don't look like a cowboy anymore."

Mouse's head came up between their seats as she looked at Billy. "You look normal now," she said.

"There's more to a cowboy than just his clothes," said Billy, sounding miffed.

"Don't worry about it," said Mouse, "you look adorable," which made Suzanne laugh.

"What about you?" Billy asked her. "You think I look adorable, too?"

"Mom likes older men," said Mouse from the back seat.

Suzanne was a little surprised to hear that as she hadn't known Mouse had any opinions on the subject. "Where'd you get that idea?" she asked her daughter.

"Every man you've ever dated has been old."

Suzanne said to Billy, "She makes it sound as though I dated a lot, which isn't true. The hours I worked I didn't have time to date and by the weekends I'd be exhausted."

"And drag me to museums," said Mouse.

"And added some culture to your life, yes."

"What about Neil?" said Mouse. "Neil was old."

"Neil wasn't any older than forty," said Suzanne. "He was just bald, that's all."

"And Charlie and Howard and Phil?"

"You got around, I guess," said Billy.

"Don't pay any attention to her," said Suzanne. "Charlie's my accountant and Howard's my business manager and they're both married. Which is the story of your life if you're a single woman my age in New York: all the good men are married."

"And Phil?" Mouse persisted.

"I used to run with Phil, that's all."

"What do you mean, run?" asked Billy.

"I mean run. As in running for exercise. Phil and I trained for the marathon together."

"Mom finally finished one," said Mouse. "For two years straight she conked out at the nineteen-mile marker, but last year she finished. She didn't come in first, though."

"I didn't even come in a hundredth."

"Well, you and Phil used to be together an awful lot. I thought you were attracted to him."

"I'm surprised you're that obtuse," said Suzanne. "Phil happens to be gay."

There was a long silence while Mouse digested that piece of information, then she said, "I didn't know that."

"Obviously," said Suzanne.

"Well, you never said."

"It wasn't pertinent."

"Does this mean you didn't date?" asked Billy.

"All it means is that Mouse isn't as smart as she thinks she is. And I don't feel like having my dating habits or lack of them discussed. Why don't you ask him about his, Mouse?"

"What do people do on dates in Wyoming, Billy?"

"Probably about the same as they do in Colorado."

"Yeah, but I haven't been to Colorado yet. Come on, let me know what I'm getting into."

"What exactly do you want to know?" asked Billy. "What my dates are like in Wyoming or what it's like to date at college? Make up your mind, because they're two distinctly different things."

"Which is more interesting?" asked Mouse.

"College. Definitely," said Billy.

Mouse giggled. "Is dating in Wyoming that boring?"

"You want to hear how boring it is?" said Billy. "I got maybe three choices of places where I can meet women. I can go to church socials, only most of the available women there are elderly widows or teenagers; I can go to the one bar in town, only that's my daddy's hangout and he's more popular with the women there than I am; or I can hang around the bus depot and hope some unlucky female tourist gets off by mistake and I can pick her up. Hell, I met more available women in the operating room than I've met in Wyoming in the past year."

"Is it really that bad?" asked Mouse.

"Worse," said Billy. "Much worse."

"It sounds like paradise to me," said Suzanne. "No singles bars; no one trying to pick you up at the health club; no personal ads. Just a quiet life with no hassles."

"You'd be bored to death in one week," said Mouse.

"I didn't always live in the city, Mouse. I think I could adjust to more normal living conditions again."

"I guess you can adjust to anything if you have to," said Billy. "I was even adjusting to that damn hospital, which made me realize it was time to get out."

"Billy has a twin sister, did you know that, Mouse?"

"You're kidding! That's great! Does she look just like you?"

"If she looked just like me she'd be a twin brother."

"You know what I mean."

"Near enough. Up until age twelve we could still fool people, then she started to get a little rounder and I started to get a little skinnier, and those days were over."

"Does she date?" asked Mouse.

"Well, she has it a little better than I do because there're a lot more available men in Wyoming than there are women."

"You hear that, Mom?" asked Mouse.

"I'm not looking for a man, Mouse."

"Yeah, but you and your friends in New York were always complaining that there were more women than men. You ought to call Abbie and Jaime and tell them to head for Wyoming."

"Actually, I talked to Abbie last night," said Suzanne.

"How's she doing?" asked Mouse.

"The same as when we left."

"Did you tell her about my accident?"

"Since it was the most interesting thing that's happened to us...."

Mouse leaned forward and spoke to Billy. "Our apartment building in New York is just like a small town: everyone knows everyone else's business. And my mom had these three women friends who told each other everything."

"Not everything," said Suzanne. "But Abbie, Jaime and Marielle are good friends."

"Did you tell Abbie about meeting a cowboy?" asked Mouse.

"I might have mentioned it."

Mouse let out a hoot. "My mom's playing it cool, Billy. She used to drag me to every cowboy movie that came to New York. She and all her friends had a thing about cowboys."

"I don't think Billy's interested in hearing this, Mouse."

Billy grinned. "I'm always glad to hear we have a popularity outside of Wyoming. It's kind of warming."

Mouse leaned forward and spoke in a hushed voice. "My mom even had a life-size poster of Clint Eastwood dressed like a cowboy on the front of her closet door. A grown woman, can you believe it?"

"That's enough, Mouse!"

"Well, you did!"

"It's not like I went out and bought it. Marielle bought it for me as a joke and I put it up so her feelings wouldn't be hurt."

Mouse giggled. "I'm surprised you didn't put a personal ad in the *Voice* saying you wanted to meet a cowboy."

"That's enough, Mouse!"

"Well, it's one way to meet a man."

Suzanne looked over at Billy. "For some reason my daughter has gotten the idea in her head that I need a man. Forget that I brought her up all by myself; now that I'm finally free of all responsibilities, she'd like nothing better than to see me lose that freedom to some man. And since you happen to be male, and somewhat trapped in this car with us, I'm sure her little mind is churning with possibilities. Just ignore her."

"I didn't say that," said Mouse. "Billy's too young for you, anyway. But doesn't Wyoming sound like a good possibility?"

"I'm not all that young," said Billy.

"You're not only young," said Suzanne, "you're helpless."

"You're not looking to get married again?" asked Billy.

"I'm planning on taking up where I left off when I had Mouse. And this time I'm going to do it differently."

"She's sorry she had me," said Mouse.

"You know I've never been sorry I had you," said Suzanne. "You've been the best thing in my life. It's your father I'm sorry about."

"Mom's going to be an adventurer now. She's going to be a free spirit and do whatever she wants."

"And right now I want to throw you out of the car, Mouse. If you want to talk, talk about yourself."

With that, Mouse subsided into silence.

Chapter Six

Suzanne said, "Okay, folks, you got a choice. We can stop early this side of Chicago, we can visit the big city, although really, I don't think any of us are dressed for it; or we can try to make it through Chicago during rush hour."

"Or we can bypass Chicago altogether," said Billy.

"Not really. Not without losing a lot of time."

"Are we in a hurry?"

"I'll tell you something, Mom, this has been a really boring day. No lookout points, you haven't let me drive once, and these seats back here are about three times as uncomfortable as the ones in the front."

"I can sit back there," said Billy.

"No," said Mouse, "you stay where you are. I just think we could stop early, take a swim in the pool, you know, act like we're on a vacation. What's the big hurry? I'm going to be in Colorado all year."

"Okay," said Suzanne, "that all right with you, Billy?"

"Great. I've got to practice my walking anyway."

"But not some little place like last night," said Mouse. "Let's at least find a town with a movie theater."

Suzanne did better than that. She found a town with a triple theater complex, a bowling alley and at least half a dozen restaurants. What's more, the first motel they came to had a pool with a slide going into it, the sight of which entranced Mouse.

Trying to check in was another thing altogether. The owners, an older couple who ran the office, gave the three of them wary looks when they entered. Still, they were polite at first, welcoming them and saying they had several vacancies, but when Suzanne asked for two rooms, the woman said, "You folks a family?"

"No," said Suzanne, getting out her gold card and setting it on the counter. She refused to be intimidated by small-town morality.

"Mom and I are sharing a room," said Mouse, putting her arm around Suzanne's waist and letting the owners get a good look at their strong resemblance.

"I'm just someone they picked up in the last town," said Billy with a big smile. Suzanne had the feeling he was identifying with these people, that he thought he had more in common with them than with her and Mouse.

The couple exchanged a meaningful look and the woman's mouth pursed up. The man cleared his throat. "You folks might be happier at the Wayfarer Inn," he said, the meaning clear that he thought the next roadside inn was less particular about whom they rented to.

"I'm sure we'll be happier here," said Suzanne. "My daughter admires your water slide."

"The Wayfarer Inn could give you a suite," said the woman.

"We don't require a suite," said Suzanne. "We'd like a double and a single, preferably close to each other."

She could sense the advent of the first skirmish when the man began to tear up her registration card. "Are you refusing to give us rooms?" she asked him.

"Wayfarer Inns are pretty nice," said Billy. "I stayed in one once where they had a preacher on call."

"We're not going to require a preacher, either," said Suzanne.

"I don't really need to slide, Mom," said Mouse. "It's probably only for little kids anyway."

"They have a lounge over there, too," said the man. "We don't serve liquor here."

"Well, that settles it," said Billy. "I mean, if we can't drink, what's the point?"

"This place gives me the creeps, Mom."

Suzanne reached up and pulled off her sunglasses with one hand and her hat with the other. With a vapid smile and a soft drawl, she said, "I had my heart set on the Nighty-Night Motel."

The man's mouth dropped open as the woman clutched her chest. The woman was the first to speak. "Dad, it's Barbara Jean."

She was getting out a new registration card and shoving it across the counter at Suzanne as the man regained control of the muscles around his mouth and said, "We can put a sign up in the lobby saying Barbara Jean slept here. Would you folks mind posing for a picture? I have my Polaroid back in our apartment, it'll only take me a minute to get it."

Suzanne's sweet smile vanished. "What do you say, guys, you think we'd be happier at the Wayfarer Inn?"

"Definitely," said Mouse.

"Without a doubt," said Billy.

"Then let's get this show on the road," said Suzanne, turning around and heading for the door. She ignored the entreaties to stay from the couple at the desk as she and Mouse swept out the door. Their exit was somewhat spoiled by the fact that Billy dropped one of his crutches on the way and Mouse had to go retrieve it for him, and then they were all laughing so hard they had to stop in the parking lot for a minute to catch their breath.

"You were great, Mom," said Mouse.

"I guess Barbara Jean comes in real handy at times," said Billy.

"Not in New York," Suzanne told him. "If it had worked miracles like this in New York, I might not have left."

BILLY CAREFULLY LOWERED HIMSELF onto the chaise longue, set his crutches down on the ground and propped his book on his stomach. Several tourists, their bodies well-oiled, were occupying the other chaises. Billy was wearing Suzanne's shorts and an Ace bandage on his leg. The leg with the bandage looked better than the other leg because the other leg was pasty white, as were some other parts of his body. His face and neck were tan, the lower parts of his arms were tan, and the rest of him looked practically albino. Ranchers did not, however, do their work shirtless and he was not going to apologize for it. He just wished that it were possible to acquire a tan before Suzanne appeared at the pool.

When she did appear, there was a stir of interest around the pool. The men were surreptitiously—and not so surreptitiously—eyeing Suzanne's body, and the women, for the most part, recognized her instantly. He heard some whispers of "Barbara Jean," but no one shouted out to her or made a fuss. Maybe the people staying at the Wayfarer Inn were a more sophisticated group.

Billy was looking at Suzanne's body, too. Not that he hadn't seen most of it before, but her bikini was even skimpier than her everyday clothes. The top covered her pretty well; the bottom covered her hardly at all. There was a patch in the front, a couple of strings, and another patch in the back. He had a hard time believing such a suit was legal.

Suzanne ignored the looks, ignored the whispers, ignored him and headed straight for the diving board. She poised at the end of it for a moment, then executed a clean dive into the water.

Twenty laps later Billy gave up watching her in exhaustion. Then Mouse showed up. Same bikini, same coverage, but somehow cute on her rather than sexy. Mouse waved to him and then jumped in the pool holding her nose.

Billy felt parts of him starting to burn by the time he looked up from his book and saw Suzanne dragging a chaise over next to his.

"Too bad you can't go in the water, it feels great," she said, shaking some of the water out of her hair and getting him wet.

She adjusted the chaise so that it lay flat, then positioned herself on her stomach. The next thing he knew she was reaching around and untying the back of her bikini top.

"You think you ought to do that?" asked Billy, looking around to see if anyone was going to call the police.

"Do what?"

"Take your top off. I have a feeling this isn't a place where you can go topless. In fact I've never even seen one. I've heard about them, of course, but I've never actually been to one."

"I have no intention of going topless," said Suzanne. "I'm hardly an exhibitionist."

This was news to Billy.

"I'm just untying it so that I don't get a mark on my back."

"Well, don't sit up all of a sudden," said Billy, hoping that she'd do that very thing.

"How's the book?"

"Scary."

"He's Mouse's favorite writer; I think she's read everything he's written."

"He has a way with words, all right. You can have it when I'm finished."

"I never read fiction."

"Where I live, there's not much else to do."

"No TV?"

"The reception's almost as bad as the programs."

"Sounds like my kind of place. Probably no one's ever heard of Barbara Jean there."

"I wouldn't count on that," said Billy. "A lot of folks have these big dishes that pick up the stations. I just don't happen to think it does a hell of a lot for the scenery. The reception in town's not bad, though."

"If it's none of my business, just say so, but is your father an alcoholic?"

Billy almost fell off the chaise. "My daddy? Where'd you get that notion?"

"What you said about him hanging out in the town's one bar."

"Oh, hell, no. He puts a few away, but he doesn't have a drinking problem. No, his problem is he's something of a celebrity."

"Another Barbara Jean?"

"Worse. He's the only one in town."

"A cowboy celebrity?"

"Daddy's no cowboy. Me and Wendy, we're the only ones in the family who ranch. He owns the only radio station in the area and has a nightly program. One of those talk shows where people call in. At one time or another Daddy's argued with everyone over the air within a hundred-mile radius."

"How did you get into ranching?"

"Growing up with my father made you long for a little piece and quiet. Daddy's just not happy unless he's in an argument."

"Your mother doesn't mind the arguing?"

"Once we were grown, Mom got a job as a game warden and cut out. She comes home once in a while, but most of the time she lives in her cabin."

"What an interesting family."

"What about your folks?"

"They live in Minnesota."

"Minnesota? You mean you weren't big-city born and bred?"

"I didn't grow up on a farm, but I'm not from New York, if that's what you mean."

"So how come you're not headed north to see them?"

"Mouse already spent a week with them this summer, and I thought I'd stop by after I dropped her at college. I'm going to drive around and see the whole country."

"So how'd you get from Minnesota to New York?"

"Are you asking me to bore you with the sad story of my life?"

"Just the good parts."

"Well, I was in my first year of college, it was in the spring, and this rock group came to play on campus. Not a big name or anything, but they were good. I fell in love with the bass guitarist, who also wrote their songs, and when they headed to New York to find fame and fortune, I ran off with him.''

''Sounds pretty romantic.''

''Oh, it was very romantic. It was probably the fulfillment of every high-school fantasy I ever had. It went along fine for a while. We got married, all of us lived together in this big apartment on the Lower East Side, and they actually got some gigs in some of the clubs. Then the lead singer decided to go off on his own, the drummer got a job with a better-known group, and I got pregnant. Basil decided—''

''Basil?''

''He called himself Sweet Basil. Anyway, he decided marriage and a pregnant wife were stifling his creativity, and he and the keyboard man took off for Europe. The last I heard he was living in Greece.''

''So why didn't you go home to your folks?''

''Lots of reasons. Pride. Wanting to be independent. Not wanting to hear my parents tell me 'I told you so' the rest of my life. But mostly I was enjoying New York. There's something very energizing about that city, particularly when you're young. And I did it. I made out all right. Doesn't Mouse seem okay to you?''

''She's fantastic. You did a great job on her.''

''Well, she did a lot of that herself. She was just a naturally sensible child from the start.''

Billy saw that the naturally sensible child was now having a water fight in the pool with a bunch of twelve-year-olds. He figured it was probably a big comedown for her after her date the night before.

''You've sure led a more interesting life than I have.'' Billy told her.

''But you're doing what makes you happy, that's what's important. Anyway, I've lived longer.''

"Can we get this straight right now? You're only two years older than me, Suzanne, which is hardly what I'd call a chasm between us."

"It's not the age difference so much, Billy. There's something very young and innocent about you."

"And you're the experienced woman from New York."

"It makes a difference. I'd be a different person today if I'd stayed in Minnesota."

Billy glanced over at the pool in time to see a very strange sight. That trooper, Daryl, the one who had been out with Mouse the night before, was dropping from the wall that surrounded the pool area and landing behind the shrubbery.

Billy thought of mentioning it to Suzanne, then decided against it. He'd leave it up to Mouse to tell her mother the police had arrived.

MOUSE WAS HANGING onto the edge of the pool and kicking her feet when she saw something red moving behind the shrubbery. She watched it for a moment, then saw a hand move between two bushes and beckon to her.

Too much Stephen King, thought Mouse, looking away to see if anyone else had noticed. She was now seeing bogeymen in the bushes.

What she saw next wasn't the bogeyman, although it was just as unexpected. For a brief second the bushes were parted and she saw Daryl's face grinning out at her.

Daryl? In the bushes? At the Wayfarer Inn? Mouse blinked, wondering if it was possible to get sunstroke from a few minutes in the pool. Or hallucinations from drinking too much caffeine.

She squinted to get a better look, but the face had disappeared. If it was the bogeyman making her think it was

Daryl, she wasn't going to fall for it. If it was a hallucination she didn't want to know about it. But if it was Daryl, then what was she waiting for?

Mouse looked around and saw her mother and Billy deep in conversation. She pulled herself up over the side of the pool, adjusted the bottom of her bikini and casually strolled over to the hedge.

"Is that you, Daryl?" she whispered loudly. Who cared if the kids in the pool thought she was talking to herself?

"Can you meet me in the parking lot?" Daryl whispered back.

"What're you doing here?"

"Hurry up," said Daryl, "I'm getting eaten alive by gnats."

Mouse wrapped the hotel towel around her waist and slowly sauntered out of the pool area as though heading for her room. As soon as she got out of view of her mother, she broke into a run. She met Daryl at the entrance to the parking lot, which was lucky for her as the parking lot was blacktop and she was barefooted.

He held out his arms and she ran into them, practically babbling in delight. "You followed me here? Did you actually follow us? Did they let you off work?"

"I've been following you all day," said Daryl. "I was real relieved when you stopped early. What happened at that first motel you stopped at?"

"Never mind that, I can't believe you actually followed me."

"Oh, hell, Mouse, I couldn't let you go like that. I mean, I finally met the perfect woman, I sure wasn't going to let you get away."

Mouse basked for a minute in the knowledge that he not only thought of her as a woman, he also thought she was perfect. "Can you just take off work like that?"

"I quit."

"You quit your job? For me?" This was clearly the most romantic thing that was ever likely to happen to her.

"I had some money saved and I've got my pickup and I figure I can manage for a few months. At first I was just going to take my sick time, but then I figured, what the hell!"

"Daryl, my mom's never going to let me go off with you. She's driving me to college!"

"I'm not asking you to go off with me, Mouse. Hell, I don't figure we know each other all that well yet. I just want the chance to get to know you on the road. You can get out at night, can't you?"

"I'll make sure I can. It'll be a lot easier with Billy along, Mom will have something to do."

"Fate's sure a funny thing, Mouse. If you hadn't knocked that cowboy's car over the cliff, we never would've met."

"You have a room here?" she asked him.

"I sure do. Room 239."

"Let me get dressed, figure out what to say to Mom, and I'll meet you there."

Daryl's arms tightened around her for a moment. "Don't be too long, honey, it's been a real long day."

MOUSE DIDN'T LIKE lying to her mother but she didn't feel she had a choice. She knew that Suzanne would be less than thrilled that Daryl was now following them across the country. She would also be suspicious. Her mother might be naive, but she wasn't stupid. She was pretty sure her mother would deduce that more had gone

on between her and Daryl than a little fun with his friends
to make him up and quit his job and follow Mouse to the
ends of the earth. Well, to Colorado, anyway.

All her life she had heard from her mother about the
stupid mistake she had made in leaving college and running off with Mouse's father. All her life her mother had
been telling her how important it was to have a college
education; how necessary it was for a woman to have a
profession so that she was able to support herself. And
her mother was not going to believe that Daryl was following her because he was interested in seeing Mouse go
to college. As far as that went, Mouse wasn't interested
in going to college. She was going for the freedom and to
meet boys and to get in some skiing while she was at it,
but as for going to learn some profession, forget it.
Mouse wanted to live life, not learn about it.

Still, she didn't like lying to her mother. She did it, but
she didn't like it. And when she did it it was always for
her mother's good, for her peace of mind. Like telling her
mother she was going to Jones Beach with her friend's
parents instead of admitting she was taking the subway
out to Coney Island. Or telling her mother she was at the
Museum of Natural History when she was actually sun-
bathing in Central Park. Or telling her mother she was at
the neighborhood movie theater when she was at Madison Square Garden at a rock concert. Rock concerts were
the worst. Since her mother had met her father at a rock
concert, Suzanne was in constant fear that Mouse would
go to a concert and Sting would magically see her from
the stage, fall in love with her and carry her off. Like that
really was going to happen!

Forget that she had grown up in a tough city, her mom
still thought of her as a helpless baby. She was just surprised her mother was actually allowing her to go off to

college. She had her suspicions about that, though. She had this idea that Suzanne was going to settle down in Colorado and begin to hint that Mouse could go to college while still living at home. She wouldn't put it past her.

So she had to lie. She really did. But she didn't like it.

BILLY WAS ALREADY SEATED at the bar when Suzanne walked in. He was wearing his shorts, which surprised her. Maybe he had noticed that most of the men staying at the motel were wearing shorts. Or maybe he couldn't get his pants on by himself. He looked different every time he changed his clothes. Now he looked like a young athlete who had hurt his leg in some sport. He had given himself a close shave, had unsuccessfully tried to wet down his hair, and his lopsided grin was hugely appealing.

She took the bar stool next to him. "Have you been waiting long?"

"A beer and a half," said Billy. "Where's Mouse?"

"She met some kids in the pool and is going to the movies with them. Unless you have your heart set on a movie, I thought we could go shopping, pick you up a few things."

"You planning on coordinating my wardrobe, Suzanne?"

"You planning on wearing that smelly shirt the entire trip?"

Billy laughed out loud. "I'm perfectly capable of washing out my shirt in the sink at night."

"I hear there's a nice mall in town. I thought we could have dinner there, buy you a few clothes—"

"And start a stampede when everyone at the mall recognizes their beloved Barbara Jean."

Suzanne sighed. She was getting a little tired of it herself. If she were a skilled actress like Meryl Streep, she wouldn't mind being recognized. People would treat her with the respect she deserved. But being recognized as that silly, mealymouthed Barbara Jean? That was humiliating.

"I was thinking I could get my hair dyed."

"Over my dead body."

"What do you care what color my hair is, Billy?"

"Couldn't you just get a wig?"

"In this heat? I'd die underneath a wig."

"What color were you thinking of?"

"Gray."

Billy reacted so fast his beer went down the wrong way. "Gray!"

"Gray. I can pin it up on top of my head in a knot, get some clear glasses, and no one will recognize me."

"Am I allowed to give my opinion of this idea?"

Suzanne shrugged.

"The way I see it, a gray-haired granny in a miniskirt is going to cause more of a commotion than Barbara Jean on her best day."

"It was just a thought."

"Well, think again."

DARYL OPENED THE DOOR wearing only jeans. Mouse's eyes went from his smooth, tan chest down to his flat stomach and then further down to the way his jeans hugged his slim hips. She gave a little sigh of pleasure.

"Well, don't just stand there, come on in," he said, opening the door wide and stepping aside.

Mouse took a careful step into the room. This was now adult ground she was treading. Never in her wildest dreams had she thought she'd be in a motel room with a man. At least not on this trip with her mother.

"Where'd you tell your mom you were going?"

"To the movies with some kids I met at the pool."

He took her by the hand and led her over to the bed, but halfway there she veered to the right and sat down in a chair. She was feeling a little nervous, a little shy. But she relaxed when he sprawled on the bed on his stomach, his arms crossed and his chin resting on one forearm. The bed just seemed to be a place to relax to him. For her it had more serious connotations.

"So what do you want to do, see a movie?"

"I don't care," said Mouse.

"We could take a drive, do anything you want."

"We've been driving all day."

"Well, what do you want to do?"

"I don't care," said Mouse. "What do you want to do?"

"Now don't get excited."

"I'm not getting excited."

"What I was thinking," said Daryl, his eyes having a real glow to them, "was that we could order in something from room service and then watch a movie on TV. They have free HBO here."

It was just like a movie. Room service in a motel room with a man. "That sounds great," she said.

"We could even have some champagne."

"Not enough to get me drunk, though," said Mouse. "Mom would be real suspicious if I staggered in."

"I don't want you drunk," said Daryl, a slow smile creeping up on his lips.

Mouse was beginning to wish she hadn't sat in the chair. Now it seemed presumptuous to get up and walk over to the bed where she could be near him.

"Hey. Why don't you come over here and give me a kiss?"

"Why don't you tell me how much you missed me?"

"Does it need telling? Would I have quit my job and followed you if I hadn't missed you?"

"Oh, Daryl, I honestly thought I'd never see you again. I was depressed all day just thinking about it."

"This is something else, isn't it? I mean, who'd of thought we'd meet like this and feel this way about each other? What are you sitting all the way over there for?" He got off the bed and walked over to her, reaching down one hand to help her out of the chair.

And then she was in his arms and her earlier depression was only a memory as his lips closed over hers. Mouse was so glad she was finally an adult.

"YOU LOOK TERRIFIC," said Suzanne, standing back and looking him over.

Billy took a look at himself in the full-length mirror. "Khaki shorts, a white shirt, running shoes—what're you trying to do, make me look like some prep-school type?"

"Buy cowboy clothes, I don't care," she said, turning away and looking over a selection of cotton sweaters.

Billy looked around the men's store. "Sure, you say that knowing full well they don't carry western clothes."

"You don't need to buy anything," said Suzanne. "Mouse and I have enough clothes you can borrow."

"Yeah, but except for those little skirts, your clothes look just like these." He really didn't feel like arguing, though. His leg was tiring fast and he'd rather be eating dinner with Suzanne than trying on clothes.

He told the clerk he'd wear what he had on, then picked out some boxer shorts, a few pairs of socks, a new pair of jeans that already were soft and looked used and half a dozen plain T-shirts. Then like the helpless cripple he was, he had to ask Suzanne to carry the shopping bag for him because he couldn't manage it with his crutches.

He noticed that she had to make a concerted effort to slow her walk down to his pace as they walked through the mall. She was also opening doors for him and moving in to protect him with her body when kids ran past. Hell, she was acting like a man. The one woman he'd like to impress, and instead he was powerless to do anything but let her watch out for him. It sure didn't do much for his self-image.

They passed a sporting-goods store and Suzanne stopped to look in the window. Billy didn't look. Sports weren't anything he was going to be able to do anymore, not that he had before the accident. But once the doctor had told him he'd never be able to play tennis or ski again, even though Billy had never done either of them, he developed this unreasonable desire to try both.

"Are you supposed to be exercising your leg?" Suzanne asked him.

"I'm going to have to see a physical therapist when I get home."

"What about before then?"

"I've got some exercises I do."

"Well, if you need any help with them, let me know."

Billy pictured himself lying flat on the bed while she helped him bend his ankle the way the therapist in the hospital had done. He decided he didn't like the picture. "Unless you want to go in there, I could sure use some food."

"I'm eating too much and not exercising enough. Sitting in that car all day isn't going to do me any good, and I haven't been getting up early enough to run."

"As I recall, you swam so many lengths I lost count."

"Yes, but I didn't yesterday or the day before. I'm half tempted to get one of those folding exercycles. Would you be able to use it, too?"

"They had me on one in the hospital, but I couldn't get my leg to go around once."

"I'm going to get one," said Suzanne, heading into the store.

Billy couldn't see it. Riding a real bike, sure, it took you somewhere, the same way a horse did. But riding one that didn't go anywhere? Just for the fun of it? It sounded like a big waste of time.

He'd give it a try, though. It was one of the things the physical therapist had recommended. It was another thing she'd have to help him with, though, because he couldn't even get up on the seat by himself.

When she came back out with an exercycle under her arm, she said, "Why don't we go back to the motel and order in room service? I'd like to give this a try."

"I need to be fed instantly, woman."

"You look like you're ready to drop."

"I am. Into a chair, in front of a table piled with food. We cowboys have appetites, ma'am."

She gave him a doubtful look, then spotted some benches around a fountain. She led him to one of the benches and said, "Wait for me while I put the exercycle in the car. Then we'll get you fed."

Billy watched the women in the mall until she got back. He couldn't find one that held a candle to Suzanne. They didn't have her looks, they sure didn't have her style, and she was the only one who looked as though she was really enjoying life.

He liked that about her, the fact that she seemed open to new experiences. Anyone else with a high-paying job like she had would just stick with it and pile up the money. Maybe put some aside for retirement one day. But not her. Here she was, setting out on a new life, not content to settle for security. He thought she'd get along just fine in Wyoming. She had the kind of adventurous style that people in his state admired. The kind he admired.

He wondered what his family would think if he showed up back home with a New York City woman. His daddy would be admiring, he could be sure of that. His daddy had an eye for a pretty woman and the patter to go with it. In fact, he'd have to watch her around his daddy.

His mom would love her. He thought Suzanne and his mom would have a lot in common. His mom had that same kind of spirit, going out when her kids were grown and finding a new, more exciting life for herself. Both had had early marriages that were not ideal, but Suzanne had survived hers and gone on to make a good life for her daughter, and his mom had stuck with hers and acted as a sane buffer between the kids and their father.

Wendy, though; Wendy was going to be a problem. Wendy had this idea that she was king of Wyoming. Not queen. Wendy was too tough to see herself as any kind of queen. Wendy was going to go into action the minute she caught sight of Suzanne, but Billy had the feeling that if he pitted the two of them against each other, it would come out a draw. Wendy might think she knew everything, but she'd never been out of Wyoming in her life and Suzanne had had to come up against more adversity in the big city than Wendy had ever had to contend with.

Yeah, the two of them meeting up would be something else. And he was going to do everything in his power to make sure it happened. Now that he'd met the woman of his dreams, there was no way he was going to let her get away.

SUZANNE SAW BILLY'S SMILE when he spotted her entering the mall and quickened her pace. She would get him a good meal, then go back to the motel and make sure he did his exercises. Oh, God, she was beginning to sound motherly, and that wasn't how she felt about him at all. She guessed it had something to do with the fact that she'd spent ninety-nine percent of her time in the last years being a mother and only one percent of it dating men.

Not that this was a date, but it felt nice hanging out with a man again, particularly one as easy to get along with as Billy. He had none of the annoying mannerisms of New York men: he wasn't into health, he wasn't into success, he wasn't concerned with status.

"What do you feel like eating?" she asked him. "I saw a steak place, an Italian restaurant and they even have a sushi place, although where they get the fish I can't imagine."

Billy pulled himself up with his crutches. "Not the last one, whatever that is."

"The steak place is probably our best bet."

"I can always eat a good steak," said Billy.

"Mouse should've come with us," said Suzanne. "She'll probably only have popcorn in the movies."

"Popcorn's sometimes enough when you're a kid."

"I guess she needs to be with other kids once in a while."

She held the door for Billy to enter the restaurant, then she went inside and took a look at one of the menus. It amazed her how much food you could get for so little once you were out of the city.

They were seated at a table and the waiter held out her chair for her, but Suzanne ignored him and instead held out Billy's chair, then arranged his crutches so that they wouldn't fall on the floor. Then she saw his expression and said, "I'm sorry, I'm making you feel helpless, aren't I?"

"A little," said Billy, "but I'll survive the experience. I can't imagine you having to do that for Clint Eastwood, though."

"Is that how you see yourself? The lone cowboy, dependent on nobody?"

"I'd like to see myself that way," said Billy, "but it wouldn't be true. It'd also be damn lonely."

"I don't know," said Suzanne. "Being alone doesn't have to be lonely. I think I could like it."

"It seems to me you've been alone for quite some time."

"You're not alone when you have a child."

"I have a sister, but it's not the same as having someone all to myself."

"Why aren't you married?" Suzanne asked him.

"If you slow down the words when you say that, you'll sound exactly like my mother."

"You don't seem the type not to be married."

"Nor do you."

"But I was married once."

"I don't know; there never seemed to be time. It takes time to go out and find someone, get to know her, all of that. Trying to get a ranch going, at least up until the last couple of years, was a seven-days-a-week, twenty-four-hours-a-day proposition. When I had some free time, all I wanted to do was sack out."

"And the last couple of years?"

Billy shrugged. "You'd have to see where I live to understand, but the women all disappeared. It's not like New York where you can walk out on the street any day of the week and pass maybe a million men you hadn't seen before. By the time I had time to look around, all the women I had gone to school with were married with kids, and the younger ones had headed for the cities. You know how rough it is to find a woman in Wyoming? I've heard of a couple of guys who purposely corresponded with Oriental women and then brought them over to the States to marry them.''

''Maybe you should have stayed in New York longer. There are a lot of women there who would love to meet a cowboy.''

''No, you're wrong, Suzanne. I think I left at exactly the right time.''

''Don't start getting any ideas, Billy.''

''You're a little too late with your warning.''

''I think what we should do, Billy, is get you fed and then back to the motel so you can rest that leg.''

''You trying to come across as a mother, Suzanne?''

''It's not working?''

Billy slowly shook his head.

DARYL LOOKED DOWN AT HER. ''Oh, God, Mouse, I love you so much. Just looking at that face of yours makes me happy.''

''I feel the same way.''

''Say it.''

Mouse, a little shyly, said, ''I love you, Daryl. I know it's soon and all, but I really do.''

''I guess it happens like this sometimes.''

''It always does in movies.''

''You're not just teasing me, are you? Just leading me on until you meet some college men?''

''Oh, no. I don't think I could meet anyone else I'd feel this way about. It's crazy the way you're from Ohio and

I'm from New York but we're so much alike. I feel like this was meant to be."

"Me, too. That's why I followed you. I knew if I let you drive out of my life that would be it. I'd never feel the same way about anyone else, ever."

He moved over her, his face just inches from hers, and slowly began to lower his body.

Mouse got up her nerve to ask, "Are you using a condom, Daryl?"

"Come again?"

Mouse avoided his eyes. "I'm sure even in Ohio they have condoms."

Daryl, looking perplexed, moved to her side on the bed. "Sure we have them, but aren't you on something?"

This was terrible, this was just awful. She wanted more than anything in the world to make love to him, and now she knew they were going to have an argument instead. *"On* something? You mean like drugs?"

"I didn't mean that, Mouse. I mean, don't you take birth-control pills or anything? I figured being from New York and all . . ."

"No, Daryl, I'm not on something. And the reason I'm not is I've never done this before."

"Oh, hell, Mouse, you telling me you're a virgin?"

"There still are such things as virgins in New York, Daryl. And even if I were on something, I'd still want you to use a condom. This is the eighties, in case you hadn't heard. It's safe sex or no sex."

"Safe? What do you think, I have some disease? We don't have that where I come from."

"You have something to prove it?"

"Damn, Mouse, I don't much feel like it anymore anyway."

"Well, fine. I don't feel like it, either. And you needn't bother following us anymore, either. Go back to your small town and find someone who's *on* something."

"I think I'll just do that."

"Fine. Go ahead."

"I will."

"Good." She got up off the bed, got dressed in record time and headed for the door. When he didn't stop her, when he didn't start apologizing, she opened the door, went out and slammed it behind her.

She was halfway down the corridor when his door opened and she heard him yell, "I still love you, Mouse," but she ignored him. She loved him, too, but she wasn't sure she was ready for sex. It was fun when it was spontaneous, but all that talk of safe sex had had its effect on her, too. It really lost the excitement when you had to stop and talk about it first.

But what else was she supposed to do? She wasn't on anything and she didn't want to get pregnant any more than she wanted AIDS. What she was going to have to do was talk to some of the other girls at college about it and find out what they did. It was for sure she couldn't talk to her mother about it because back in the old days when her mother was still having a sex life there wasn't any imminent danger involved, and if her mother had known anything about birth control she wouldn't have gotten pregnant with her.

And how in the world was she going to explain to her mother that she was home from the movies so early?

Chapter Seven

"I think we'll make Kansas City today," said Suzanne, but Mouse wasn't paying attention. She was getting bored watching farms go by. The earth lay flat and she could see for miles, but all there was to see was farmland and cows. Lots of cows. The novelty of seeing her first cow had long since worn off.

She kept looking out the back window hoping to catch a glimpse of Daryl's pickup, but while there were plenty of pickups, none was Daryl's. She couldn't believe he had just given up following her.

She had wondered briefly whether he had given up because he couldn't have sex. She didn't think so, though. She thought it had more to do with her attitude. She guessed she could've been more subtle about his using protection, only she hadn't had the experience to know how to be subtle. And she had wanted to have sex just as much as he. Maybe more. After all, it would have been her first time and she had been dying to find out if it was worth all the fuss people made about it. There must be something to it or people wouldn't line up to see X-rated movies, would they?

But instead he'd given up and gone home. He'd probably get his job back and forget all about her. The idea made her miserable. How could he say he loved her and then just leave like that? Of course she had let him, and she loved him, didn't she? Of course she did. If she didn't, she wouldn't be feeling so miserable.

"This is boring," said Mouse, loud enough for her mother to hear.

"You want to stop for a few minutes?"

"No. I want to get to something interesting. I want to see a mountain or a desert or a canyon. Something we don't have in New York." And if her mother pointed out they didn't have cows in New York, she was going to barf.

"Maybe we can all do something tonight in Kansas City," said Suzanne.

"Like what?"

She saw her mother looking at Billy, but he was looking out the window. Billy probably liked seeing all the cows; they probably reminded him of home.

"We could at least go to a movie," said Suzanne.

"Big deal."

"Well, it would be a big deal to me. Let me remind you, Mouse, you've been out the last two nights. I haven't had a very exciting time of it, either."

"You had Billy."

Billy gathered his attention away from the cows and looked around at her. He had this expression on his face that made her think he knew exactly what was the matter with her, only that wasn't possible. Unless he was psychic. And she'd never heard of a psychic cowboy.

Billy said, "If you want to drive for a while, I can get back there. Being a passenger gets kind of boring."

"Can I drive, Mom?"

"I don't see why not. Next rest area I'll pull in."

At least it would be something to do. Something to take her mind off Daryl.

SUZANNE PULLED IN to the rest area and parked. When she saw Billy reach for the door handle, she said, "Don't bother, I don't mind sitting in back. I can curl up, but you wouldn't be able to with that leg brace."

She switched places with Mouse and Mouse pulled out onto the highway. Suzanne was a little leery of letting Mouse drive again, but if she didn't get some more experience she'd never have confidence as a driver. And she thought that Mouse would be extra careful with Billy in the seat beside her.

It would be a relief not to sit next to Billy for a while. Half the time he watched her and it was making her nervous. She knew he was attracted to her. She'd have to be blind not to see that. He was very cute and very endearing and she had a feeling he could also be very sexy with the right motivation, but he couldn't have picked a worse time as far as she was concerned.

She had two things on her mind right now. The first was to get Mouse to college and discharge herself of that responsibility. The second was to decide what she wanted to do with the rest of her life. What she didn't need was a brief, on-the-road romance with a cowboy. It wouldn't set a very good example for Mouse, and she didn't believe in brief flings. As far as that went, Billy wasn't in any kind of physical condition to have a brief fling even if she was amenable.

"You okay back there?" asked Billy, looking around at her.

"I'm fine," she said, but she wasn't fine. She could see why Mouse was getting bored. The only thing to look at was the cows and she had seen enough cows growing up. Her parents would take her on drives and have her amuse herself by counting cows. She couldn't remember it amusing her much in those days, either.

"I think it's time for a little harmonizing," said Billy. "Nothing like singing a few songs to brighten up a dull day on the road."

Billy began to sing a song about going to Kansas City and some memory of the words came back to Suzanne and she joined in, humming over the parts she couldn't remember. She saw Mouse looking at her in the rearview mirror, probably surprised to hear her mother singing. Suzanne couldn't ever remember singing in front of Mouse before, at least not since she was a little kid.

When they had sung it four times, each time louder and more of the words coming back to her, Mouse said, "You guys know anything more recent?"

"I kinda doubt it," said Billy, who broke into a rousing rendition of "Home on the Range." Everyone was able to sing along with that and the mood in the car seemed to lighten. Thank God for Billy. Suzanne had a feeling she and Mouse would be picking at each other by this time if Billy weren't along to keep them behaving.

BILLY WAS TEACHING THEM the chorus to "Lock Up Your Women There's Cowboys in Town" when there was a loud slapping noise and Mouse instantly panicked.

"What's wrong? The car's pulling to the right, Mom, and I'm not doing anything wrong, I swear!"

"What's that noise?" said Suzanne from the back seat.

Billy reached over and held the steering wheel steady with his left hand. "Pull off onto the shoulder," said Billy, keeping his voice calm. "Take your foot off the accelerator and let the car slow down naturally, that's right, and put your turning signal on. Not that one, the other way. Okay, now put on the brakes slowly."

"Is it a flat?" asked Suzanne.

"It's a flat," said Billy.

Mouse was near tears. "I can't do anything right! Every time I drive something goes wrong."

"It's only a flat," said Billy. "Everyone gets flats."

Mouse turned off the motor and turned around in her seat. "Do you know how to change one, Mom?"

"Well, I've never actually done it...."

Billy opened his door and began his slow exit. "Don't worry, folks, I'm an old hand at flats."

"How can you change one with your leg like that?" asked Mouse, getting out of her side and looking at the flat rear tire with horror.

Billy was disappointed that he had been looking at the tire when Suzanne got out of the car. One of the high points of his day was watching her manage that little feat in her short skirt.

Suzanne unlocked the back of the Jeep and swung the door open. "I think there's a jack in here," she said.

Billy reached in past her and pulled out the jack. "Do you think you'll be able to do what I tell you?"

"I don't see why not," said Suzanne, taking the jack from him and following his instructions.

And the jack was no problem. What was a problem was getting the tire off, and Suzanne didn't seem to be able to manage it. Mouse gave it a try, too, but whoever had put the tires on had put them on to stay.

Billy knew there was no way he was going to be able to do it. Not from a standing position, anyway. He might possibly be able to lie down on the shoulder and reach up, and he'd probably have to do just that. And then he'd feel about as ridiculous as a turtle on his back, and just as helpless. But maintaining his image really wasn't important at the moment.

He was just getting down on his good knee, his other leg stretched out in front of him, when he heard a car engine and looked around in time to see a pickup pulling onto the shoulder behind them. He also heard a gasp from Mouse.

The next thing that happened was that Trooper Daryl was getting out of the truck and giving them all the phoniest look of surprise that Billy had ever seen.

"Daryl!" Mouse managed to say, but the tone of surprise in her voice was even phonier than Daryl's smile.

And Suzanne was oblivious, as usual. "Why, Daryl, where did you come from?"

"Fancy meeting you folks," said Daryl. "I see you've run into some trouble again." Without even being asked, he bent to the tire and began to effortlessly remove it.

"What are you doing out of Ohio?" asked Suzanne. Mouse, Billy noted, wasn't asking anything. Mouse was looking half mad and half excited and didn't seem to be able to drag her eyes away from Daryl's muscular arms.

Daryl smiled up at Suzanne. "I'm taking a little vacation time," he said, "driving out west. Talk about coincidence...."

"I don't believe in coincidence," said Suzanne.

"You visiting someone out west?" Mouse asked him.

Daryl ignored her and continued to direct his remarks at Suzanne. "I just thought I'd like to see the west. You know I've never been west of Chicago? You folks, taking the trip, kind of put it in my mind." He winked at Mouse. "And, of course, falling in love with that devastating daughter of yours helped," he said with the kind of exaggeration that made lie of what he was saying.

And Billy, who knew hyperbole when he heard it, looked on in amazement as Suzanne bought the lie with a laugh.

It wasn't more than two minutes later that Daryl had the tire changed and was telling Suzanne she ought to get it fixed at the first opportunity. "I'll follow along behind you," he said, "in case you should happen to have another flat. Not that that's likely."

Suzanne turned to her daughter. "Why don't you ride along with him, honey? That way you'll have something to do besides count the cows." She turned her smile on Daryl. "We're getting a little bored with each other's company."

"I'm not bored," said Mouse, but her words were halfhearted and Billy could see she was waiting only for Daryl to second the invitation.

"Come on, Mouse," he said. "We can count cows together."

Suzanne said, "We're trying to make it to Kansas City tonight. Unless you want to go farther, why don't you stop there and let me buy you dinner? I owe you at least that for changing the tire."

"I'd be pleased to accept your offer, ma'am," said Daryl, nice and polite and making points with Suzanne.

Once back in the Suzuki, Suzanne said to Billy, "Well, what a lucky thing that was. Not that we couldn't have managed to get the tire changed, but Mouse was beginning to climb the walls. I don't think she minded, do you? She seemed to like Daryl well enough back in Ohio."

Billy felt like shaking her silly and telling her to open her eyes. All he could figure was that she had a blind spot when it came to her daughter.

"I FIGURED YOU'D BE BACK in Ohio by now," said Mouse, trying to sound indifferent while she hugged the door and stayed as far away from Daryl as possible.

"You got a lot to learn about me then. I don't give up nearly that easily."

"I'm sorry about last night. I don't think I was wrong, but I guess I could've been nicer about it. I mean I could've mentioned it sooner."

"I should be the one apologizing. I shouldn't have just taken things for granted, but I wanted you so much, Mouse. But as far as I'm concerned, we can forget about the sex if you want. I'm just happy being with you."

"I keep thinking I'll never see you again. First back in Ohio, and then today. I hate that, Daryl. If we lived in the same place it would be different, but if we fight on the road we'd just go in different directions."

"You don't see me going in a different direction."

"But you might next time."

"Then we've got to make sure there isn't a next time, don't we? We shouldn't be fighting anyway. Hell, we're in love! Hey, come on over here next to me."

"I can't, Daryl. Mom will see us out of the rearview mirror."

"Not if I keep a car between us," said Daryl, slowing down and letting a huge truck get between them and the Suzuki. "Now come on over; I've missed you."

Mouse scooted over on the seat and Daryl's hand immediately moved to her thigh, her right thigh, which meant his arm was now resting between her breasts. "I don't know about you, but I had a rough night."

Mouse's breathing quickened. If Daryl was feeling anything like she was feeling, she didn't see how he could drive. She moved her hand over onto his thigh and felt the hard muscles beneath. This was sure more exciting than singing "Home on the Range."

"Cat got your tongue?" asked Daryl, his hand moving up under her skirt.

"I think we better do something else, Daryl."

"Like what?"

"Like singing songs."

Daryl moved his hand back to the steering wheel with a grin. "The hell of it is, you're absolutely right."

BILLY SAW THE PICKUP drop behind and let the truck between them and knew exactly what the kids were up to. Mainly because it was exactly what he'd be up to if Suzanne would give him half a chance.

At least they weren't driving in city traffic. City traffic was the worst. It really drove him berserk when Suzanne was shifting, the legs constantly moving and the skirt riding up higher and higher. And he had to get his mind off the length, or lack of it, of Suzanne's skirt or he was going to attack her. When he first thought of driving home he hadn't envisioned a long drive in a constant state of excitement. The best thing about it was that it took his mind off the pain. In fact he was beginning to think he ought to substitute the pain pills for tranquilizers.

"Want to sing some more?" he asked her.

She smiled over at him. "I thought that was for Mouse's benefit."

"Oh, I don't know; I was rather enjoying it." Meaning it might take his mind off what was uppermost in it.

"Sure, sing another; I'll sing along."

Billy started singing "Fly Me to the Moon," taking note of the look of surprise on Suzanne's face before she joined in. It wasn't exactly a cowboy song but it sure conveyed what he was feeling.

"YOU GOING TO WEAR THAT?" asked Mouse, looking at the long, straight skirt that came to her mother's ankles and the matching oversize T-shirt. It was in a soft olive green and Mouse had one just like it in a dusty pink.

"I'm getting tired of being stared at," said Suzanne, pulling her hair up on top of her head and fastening it with an orange plastic clip.

Mouse got out her pink outfit, then took another look at her mother. "You know, with a little eye makeup no one would recognize you. Particularly with your hair up."

"You think so?"

"Yeah."

"Could I borrow some?"

"Help yourself."

By the time her mom had piled on the mascara and the eyeliner and the brown eye shadow, Mouse didn't think she bore any resemblance to Barbara Jean. "You look great. Older, but kind of glamorous."

"Too much for Kansas City?"

"No, I don't think so."

"The guys will be in jeans."

"These outfits aren't dressy," said Mouse, putting a streak of pink in her hair to match her outfit. "Want to put a streak of green in your hair?"

"I'll pass on that. So, did you have fun riding with Daryl?"

Mouse was glad she had a lot of blush on because it disguised the real thing. "Yeah, he's fun to talk to. What about you and Billy? Did you mind being alone with him?"

"Not at all. He's beginning to feel like family."

"I think he'd like to be like family."

Her mother gave her a dark look. "That's not what I want to hear, Mouse."

"Just because you don't want to hear it doesn't mean it's not so. He's really falling for you, Mom."

"It's nothing more than proximity."

"He's been in just as much proximity to me but it's not me he can't drag his eyes away from."

"You're a little young for him."

"That doesn't stop a lot of men."

"What do you mean by that?"

"Just that a lot of old guys look at me, that's all. It's kind of creepy."

"You're a pretty girl."

"Sometimes you're really blind, Mom." Not that that blindness wasn't working out to her advantage with Daryl. The thing now was to figure out how she and Daryl could ditch her mom and Billy tonight.

IT ADVERTISED ITSELF as the best place for ribs in Kansas City, but Billy had had better. Still, he found his appetite returning with Suzanne fully clothed for a change. She looked older, a little mysterious, more the way he had pictured New York women looking.

He and Suzanne were on one side of the booth and Daryl and Mouse on the other. And either those two kids had the kind of good table manners that required that the hand not doing the eating be on the lap, or they were up to something over there.

"What do you think, should we all go to a movie?" Suzanne was asking.

Billy saw the stricken look in Mouse's eyes and said, "You folks go on. I'm kind of tired of sitting with my leg in one position."

Daryl glanced sideways at Mouse. "I thought maybe we could go dancing at a club. We all could," he added, looking over at Suzanne and Billy.

"Well, why don't you kids go on, then," said Suzanne. "I think I'll try to get Billy on the exercise bike tonight."

"Don't do me any favors," said Billy.

"You said the doctor told you you weren't going to get it back to normal without exercise."

"It's never going to be back to normal," said Billy. "What he said was if I don't exercise it, it'll never bend anymore than a few degrees."

"Well, you don't want that or you won't be able to ride a horse," said Suzanne.

"Yeah, Billy, you better do what she says," said Mouse.

If he hadn't known how bad Mouse wanted to be alone with Daryl, he would've given her an argument over that. Instead he put on a martyred expression and picked up another rib. If getting on the bike meant getting Suzanne in his room, then he didn't know what he had to complain about, anyway.

"You guys ought to make Colorado day after tomorrow sometime," said Daryl.

"That soon?" said Suzanne.

"Easy," said Daryl.

"I'd like to spend a couple of days there, get Mouse settled," said Suzanne.

"You don't have to get me settled," said Mouse.

"Well, a day anyway," said Suzanne. "We'll get you whatever you need for your room, and then I'll take Billy home."

"Where are you going after that?" asked Daryl.

Suzanne smiled. "Anywhere I want."

BILLY LOOKED UP with a grin when she entered his room carrying the exercycle. "I'll watch you all you want, but you're not getting me on that," he told her.

"Physical therapy time," said Suzanne, setting up the exercycle. "You've sat all day, it's time you exercised that leg."

He looked so comfortable propped up in bed against four pillows, a book open in his lap. "We intellectuals always get harassed by you exercise-nut types."

She had to smile at that. "Reading Stephen King hardly qualifies you as an intellectual." He did have that kind of look, though, with his glasses and his wild hair. He could easily be a budding Einstein or a classical conductor. Without his hat and boots he bore very little resemblance to the average cowboy. Or maybe it was just that she had never really seen the average cowboy, only the type hyped by Hollywood and Madison Avenue.

She stood by his bed and looked down at him. "Show me the exercises you're supposed to do."

"You just missed that, I already did them."

"You didn't have time to do them. It didn't take me five minutes to wash off my makeup and change into shorts."

"There's an ankle one you could help me with. I haven't had much success doing that one by myself."

"Okay, show me."

"Go down to the end of the bed."

She noticed that his left shoe was still on and she gently removed it. She saw that even something as simple as having his shoe removed was painful for him. "Okay, what do I do?"

He explained to her and she did as he said, gripping his ankle with one hand and the heel of his foot with the other, then slowly moving it from side to side.

"Hold on," he said with a wince, his face turning white. "Let me take a pain pill first." He reached for a glass of water and a bottle of pills. He was trying to be brave in front of her and his effort tugged at her heart.

Suzanne got on the exercycle and pretended not to notice. "Okay, I'll give you twenty minutes for the pill to work, but after that no more excuses."

She got on the bike and adjusted it to high tension. She wasn't crazy about exercycles. She would rather run, or even ride a bicycle. It was boring staring at a wall while getting exercise. She thought of turning the TV on to watch but Billy was already back to reading his book.

When the twenty minutes were up, she saw him watching her. "You really work the hell out of that, don't you?" he asked her.

"Let's try you on it."

"It's not going to work," said Billy.

"Just give it a try. I won't let you hurt yourself."

Billy got up off the bed, ignoring his crutches, and hopped over to the exercycle. "There's no way I'm going to be able to get on."

"Put your arm around my shoulder," she directed him, leading him over so that he could mount from the right side. "Okay, now when I count three, help me lift you up."

It didn't work the first time, but it worked the second. She took his left foot and gently placed it under the strap of the pedal, then waited while he did the same with the right. "Try to pedal," she said.

As his right foot began to revolve, his left fell off and swung free. She put it back into the strap and then held it there as he tried to make a full revolution. The knee wouldn't bend enough, though, and she finally realized there was no way he could do it.

"It's never going to work again," said Billy. "I'll probably be on crutches the rest of my life."

"You're expecting miracles, Billy; you just got out of the hospital."

"I'm not looking for miracles. All I want is to be able to ride a horse again."

"Did your doctor say you'd be able to?"

"Yeah. Maybe in six months if I did all the exercises. But if the horse falls on me again he said I could forget another knee operation."

"Do horses usually fall on you?"

He shook his head. "That was a first."

She put her arm around his waist and helped him hop off the bike, then back to the bed. "Sorry, Billy, I guess it was a little soon to get you up on the bike. Let's work on the exercises."

"You don't need to do this, Suzanne."

"Don't confine me to my room for a night of television, Billy. That was a punishment when I was a kid."

He started to smile. "Your parents punished you by making you watch TV?"

She nodded. "It is a punishment when you'd rather be out playing. I've never liked watching it since."

"Okay, sit down on the edge of the bed and I'll show you how to bend my knee. You've got to force it, and don't worry about it hurting me because it's going to hurt some."

She bent his knee for him fifty times, and by the end she could tell he was in terrible pain but he didn't once ask her to stop. And by the end his knee was bending a few degrees more than it had when they started.

She thought he was very brave. She didn't think she'd have the guts to inflict unnecessary pain on herself. "Want an ice pack on your leg?" she asked him. "Would that help?"

"It's supposed to," he said. "I hate to put you to all this trouble."

"It's no trouble. What you ought to have is a nurse traveling with you."

"I'll settle for you," Billy told her.

"THAT'S IT? That's all there is to it?"

Daryl groaned, burying his head in her neck. "Don't give me a hard time, woman."

"But there was hardly anything to it!"

"Mouse, it was the first time and we were both excited. It'll get better, I promise."

"I thought bells would ring and sirens go off. I thought my life would flash before my eyes."

"That's drowning."

"I thought it would be like that. The other stuff was more exciting."

"The other stuff is all part of it, Mouse. You're dissecting making love into separate parts."

"I know. I'm sorry. I guess I was expecting too much. I still love you, though."

"Thanks a lot."

"I mean it. I guess it was my fault, being new and all. I'll get the hang of it better as we go along."

"Well, actually it was my fault. I was just too excited, that's all. I mean, it's supposed to last more than a couple of seconds."

"I thought it was beautiful." Mouse rolled over and looked down at him, tracing his eyebrow with one finger. "Aren't we going to do it again?"

"In a few minutes."

"Let's do it now."

"Mouse, you have a lot to learn."

"I know. Teach me."

"WANT TO WATCH A MOVIE? I'm not trying to punish you or anything, but we can get a movie on the TV."

"Movies don't count as punishment," said Suzanne. "I like movies.

"Oh, I've seen this," said Suzanne, when the picture came on. "It's not very good, but you might like it."

"If it's not very good, why would I like it?"

"It's kind of funny. It's about these three guys who get stuck with a baby." She fiddled with the color for a few moments, then dragged a chair over beside his bed. "All you've missed is the party, showing they're swingers, and the part where the baby shows up at their front door."

"Come on up here and be comfortable," said Billy, dividing up the pillows and moving over on the bed.

"I'm fine."

"Come on. That chair's no good for anything but putting your shoes on."

She gave him a dubious look. "I'd get too comfortable and fall asleep."

"I won't let you fall asleep. Ah, so that's what you're afraid of. Don't look at me like that, Suzanne; I'm not going to attack you. Come on, we can watch it together like brother and sister."

"You watch TV in bed with your twin?"

"Oh, sure—you've heard about us country folk, I'm sure."

Suzanne began to smile. "Is she as devious as you are?"

"Devious? If I were really devious, Suzanne, I'd have faked having a bad leg just to get your sympathy. Just to lull you into thinking I was totally helpless. Then, when I got you real lulled, I'd attack."

"That's true. I don't know what I'm worried about," said Suzanne, getting up on the bed and making herself comfortable. "It's not as though you can actually do anything."

"I could try, though. I mean, it might kill me, but I could give it a try."

"And I could break your other leg for you."

"You New Yorkers are tough, aren't you?"

"Watch the movie."

"I'm watching it. It's not that deep that I can't watch it and talk to you at the same time. Seeing them change the baby's diaper isn't exactly riveting."

"You have VCRs where you live?"

"What's that, some newfangled invention?" When she punched him in the arm, he said, "Yeah, we have them. We even have two video stores in town."

"And you live out in the middle of nowhere?"

"That's right."

"Damn," said Suzanne. "And I was hoping there were still places in the country that were civilized. Where people talked instead of sitting in front of TV sets and rode horses instead of driving cars."

"If there are, I don't know of any. Oh, maybe you could go way up into the mountains and find a few folk who haven't let the twentieth century in yet, but it would take some hunting to find them."

"What do you do at the ranch when you're not working?"

Billy reached over and took her hand. "Don't panic, I'm just feeling neighborly."

"Nobody's panicking."

"Good. Well, let's see. I've got my loom set up, in lieu of a TV set, and I weave all my own clothes."

"You wear Levi's, Billy."

"That's only because the things I weave don't turn out to be wearable. And, of course, I bake bread; put up preserves. Go fishing for our food."

"The quintessential mountain man, is that it?"

"Absolutely."

"Seriously. Describe a typical evening for me."

Billy took a look at the movie and decided one of his typical evenings wasn't any more boring than what they were watching. "Well, we get up early, so our evenings aren't all that long."

"I know what you mean."

"We get up at dawn."

"So did I."

"Soap-opera stars don't get to sleep in?"

"I wish."

"I fix myself something to eat. Wendy's usually off somewhere, she's not around that much at night. I'm pretty good at fixing steaks and eggs. Having a cattle ranch we probably eat more beef than we ought to, but I swear it hasn't done a thing to my cholesterol."

"You being a medical authority."

"Right. So I eat. If there's a chill in the air, and there usually is, I build a fire in the front room. I do a little bookkeeping, which is the downside of ranching, and then I generally read until bedtime."

"You sound awfully settled down for a young man."

"You'd probably prefer my daddy. He parties most every night. What about you? What's your typical evening?"

"If I'm not staying home with Mouse, I might have dinner with friends. Maybe see a play. Lately I've spent a couple of evenings at Marielle's—her husband died a few months ago and left her with two small kids. She needed the company. Most of the time, though, I just fix

Mouse's dinner, clean up a little and go to bed early. Weekends are a little more exciting. I get to do the laundry, the grocery shopping, maybe take Mouse to a movie.''

''Well, maybe we could put a little excitement in your life.''

''Don't even think about it.''

Billy chuckled. He thought of leaning over and kissing her, then thought better of it, then told himself he was a fool if he didn't, and leaned over and kissed her. It was meant to be a brotherly sort of kiss so as not to scare her off, only of course it wasn't. If he had ever tried to kiss Wendy like that she would have belted him one, and justifiably.

Suzanne didn't even react much. She kept her eyes on the TV screen and allowed him the kiss, but she didn't participate.

''Okay, so it didn't light a fire in you,'' said Billy, feeling a little stupid for having tried.

''You trying to light a fire in me, Billy?''

''I wouldn't mind.''

''Well, that's not the way you light a fire. This is the way.'' She rolled over on her side and tilted his face with one hand. Then her mouth closed over his and he didn't know about her, but his fire was being lit, all right, and it was threatening to become an all-out prairie fire.

He tried to roll over so that they were facing each other, in the process forgetting for the moment about his leg, and when the first pain hit he nearly cried out.

Suzanne pulled away from him and got up off the bed. ''You're in no condition to play with fire, Billy. I don't want your leg on my conscience.''

''You wouldn't tease me like that if I weren't a cripple.''

"I wouldn't even be here with you."

"You're a hard woman, Suzanne."

"Billy, fooling around with me shouldn't be one of your priorities at the moment. Get that leg healed before you start fooling around."

"That's easy to say, but just because my leg hurts doesn't mean other parts of me aren't functioning perfectly."

"Well, I suggest you wait until *every*thing's functioning."

She leaned down, her lips tantalizingly close, hovering over his for a moment, and then moving in for the kiss. Her mouth was softly parted and he briefly felt the tip of her tongue. He reached up for her to pull her back down on the bed, but she danced out of his reach, her eyes glimmering with laughter.

"I'll tell you one thing, Billy," she said, as she headed for the door. "You're one hell of a fine kisser."

She opened the door and he yelled out, "You can't say that and just walk out."

"Sure I can," she said, opening the door and closing it behind her.

Billy settled back with a sigh, wishing she had turned off the TV before she left. She'd kissed him. That had to be progress. She'd kissed him and she thought he was a good kisser. He'd settle for that tonight. Maybe tomorrow night she'd let him prove his worth in other areas.

But oh, it was painful, wanting her so much and not being able to do anything about it. It was really painful, so painful it hurt. Or maybe it was just his leg that was hurting and he was overdramatizing.

Yeah, it *was* his leg, which meant time for another pain pill. Hell, he'd survive her teasing. And next time she wouldn't get away from him so easily.

"WHAT'D I TELL YOU?" said Daryl, raising himself up and looking into her eyes.

Mouse felt the smile spread across her face. She was feeling a little sore and very relaxed and totally satisfied. "Wow," was all she could manage.

"Did your life flash before your eyes?"

Mouse giggled. "Better."

"It was better than that?"

"It was amazing. Oh, Daryl, I have to leave and I don't want to. I want to stay here with you all night."

Daryl said, "Better get back before your mom comes looking for you."

He leaned down for a quick kiss, then got out of bed and headed for the bathroom. Mouse got up and went to look at herself in the mirror.

Her face was flushed and her hair was damp, but that could be from being out in the heat. She pulled on her bikini and skirt and was pulling her T-shirt over her head when Daryl came back in.

"You ought to wear something under that," said Daryl.

"Like what?"

"Like a bra."

"Bras are uncomfortable. Anyway, I don't need one."

She touched up her makeup. Not enough to look as though she had had to reapply it, just enough so it wouldn't look worn off. "I can't wait till tomorrow night," she said.

"I can't wait until tomorrow morning."

"We can't do anything in your truck."

"Hell, Mouse, I like to talk to you, too. It's not all just sex with me."

"I don't know, it's pretty sexy driving with you."

"You think so?"

"Yeah, I think so."

He came over behind her at the mirror and reached around, his hands going up inside her shirt and cupping her breasts. She felt a now-familiar pull in her body and pressed back against him. "I'm never going to be able to sleep tonight."

"I think you will. I think you'll be surprised how well you sleep. I'm going to be dreaming about you all night."

"Oh, Daryl," she said, turning around and hugging him close. The most romantic night of her life, and she had to go home to her mother!

Chapter Eight

"Oh, look at that; oh, I can't believe it. Daryl, have you ever seen anything that beautiful in your life?"

"It's just like something in a movie. Like pictures of Switzerland or something."

"Mom's pulling off; good, I want to get out and see this. This is Colorado, isn't it? Oh, I'm so glad we came here."

Daryl pulled off at the lookout point and parked behind the Suzuki. Daryl cut it a little close and for a moment Mouse felt a sense of déjà vu, but he didn't hit the Suzuki and it wasn't sent flying through the guardrail and the déjà vu was already fading by the time she climbed from the truck and joined her mother and Billy.

"I've never been anywhere this beautiful," her mom was saying.

Billy said, "Too picturesque, wait until you see Wyoming if you want real scenery."

Mouse said, "Isn't it gorgeous, Mom?" then realized she was freezing. "Hey, how come it's so cold? It's only August." She leaned against Daryl to get some of his body heat, then realized what she was doing and moved away. "We need some sweaters, Mom; I'll find them."

"How do you ski through something like that?" asked Daryl, looking over the heavy brush and fast-moving stream.

"I don't think this is a skiing area," said Suzanne.

"It sounds like Mouse is happy with her choice," said Billy, then, catching a curious look from Daryl, added, "it looks like a good place to go to college."

"It looked good in the brochure," said Suzanne, "but nothing like this. Oh, I love it—I'm glad there are places like this left. Is this where mountain men live, Billy?"

"If you want to take a hike up there and look for one, I'll wait for you," said Billy.

"Mountain men?" asked Mouse, handing her mother her jeans and a sweatshirt. Her mom just casually pulled the jeans up under her skirt, then pulled the skirt over her head. Billy was looking amazed at the procedure, and Mouse, laughing, followed suit. "You want a sweatshirt, Billy?" she asked him.

"Why not? I already look like some kind of tourist."

Mouse found him one of her mother's that said KNICKS across the chest, then Daryl went back to the truck and returned wearing a baseball jacket.

"I wonder if this is unusual weather," said Suzanne.

"We're liable to run into snow in the passes," said Billy. "We're in high-altitude country now."

"Let's not go all the way to Boulder today," said Mouse. "Let's stop somewhere, some little place, and go for a hike. Oh, I just love it. It's even better than Central Park."

"My daughter's a city girl," Suzanne said to the guys.

"I've never seen anything like this, either," said Daryl. "I've never even seen an ocean."

"An ocean's nothing compared to this," Mouse assured him.

"Okay, let's find a place," said Suzanne. "I'd like to go hiking, too—oh, Billy, I forgot about you."

"You guys go hiking, I'm fine. Anyway, this is nothing new to me."

Mouse saw her mom put her arm around Billy's waist and say, "Maybe we can find a wagon and I can pull you," and Billy said, "Don't do me any favors, Suzanne," and Mouse sensed something different from their voices.

What was going on? Was something going on between them she didn't know about? Just yesterday they were sounding like friends, but today they were sounding more like her and Daryl.

She must be imagining it. Her mom was way beyond that kind of stuff. Her mom was a serious person.

"OH, LOOK AT THAT, little log cabins," said Suzanne. "Shall we stop?"

"Well, hell, yes, it'll make me feel right to home," said Billy, exaggerating his drawl.

"You live in a log cabin?"

"Near enough."

Suzanne put on her right-turn signal, saw Daryl do the same and pulled into the motel. The vacancy sign was out and she hoped they'd have three cabins. Although they didn't really need three; there was no reason Billy and Daryl shouldn't share one. She didn't know why she hadn't thought of that last night.

All four of them trooped into the office, and when the man behind the desk asked how he could help them, Suzanne said, "We'd like a couple of cabins."

"A couple?" asked Mouse.

"I was just thinking, there's no reason Daryl and Billy shouldn't share. They all seem to have two beds."

"They're all doubles," said the man.

Daryl looked uneasy, and Suzanne said, "Don't worry about Billy, he won't be any problem."

For some unaccountable reason Billy was smiling, nearly laughing, in fact.

The smile faded, though, when Suzanne said, "I don't think Billy ought to be alone in a cabin. It's not like when he was in the room next to ours and could knock on the wall if he needed anything."

"I can take care of myself," said Billy.

"Maybe Daryl wants his own cabin, Mom," said Mouse, acting kind of antsy. She must be anxious to get out and hike. It made you kind of restless being closed up in a car all day. Either that or there was something going on between her daughter and Daryl that she didn't know about.

But then Daryl said, "I don't mind sharing," and Suzanne relaxed.

"I should've thought of it last night," said Suzanne. There was a big silence at that, so she said, "We'll take two doubles," to the man, and she and Daryl filled out the registration cards.

"I love it," said Suzanne, walking into the cabin and seeing the rustic furniture. It even had a little kitchen and she hoped that didn't mean there wasn't a restaurant around.

Mouse didn't seem thrilled. She looked at the two twin beds, stuck her nose in the bathroom, then headed for the door.

"Where're you going?" asked Suzanne.

"For a hike."

"Well, wait two minutes and I'll go with you. I want to check on Billy before we go, too."

"I'll meet you at their cabin," said Mouse.

Suzanne put on a long-sleeved T-shirt under her sweatshirt, then added a windbreaker. It felt like a winter's day. It would be exciting if it snowed, although not so much that it made driving difficult.

She loved Colorado already.

THERE WAS A KNOCK at the door and then Mouse burst into their cabin. Billy could see the girl was in a snit and he hoped she didn't blame him. Hell, he wasn't all that thrilled himself. If Suzanne had kissed him last night, he had conjured up all kinds of possibilities for tonight. Not likely now, though, with Daryl in the other bed.

Mouse stood by the door, her arms folded, looking from Daryl to Billy and back again.

"Sorry to cramp your style," said Billy, "but you got to admit the arrangement makes sense."

"I don't know what you're talking about," said Mouse.

"I think what he's saying is it's pretty obvious how we feel about each other," said Daryl.

Obvious? It was bordering on blatant.

"Mom doesn't know, does she?" Mouse asked Billy.

"Doesn't have a clue."

"I don't feel right about that," said Daryl. "I don't think we should be going behind your mother's back."

"I didn't hear you saying that yesterday," said Mouse, and Billy could see there was a potential for a fight brewing between them.

"Hey, don't worry about it," said Billy. "That's what parents are for. You're supposed to go behind parents' backs. That's why they have backs."

Mouse began to smile. "Oh, well, we'll be in Boulder tomorrow, won't we?"

"Unless we run into some snow," said Billy.

There was a knock on the door and when Mouse opened it, Suzanne walked in wearing more clothes than Billy would've believed she owned.

"Is there anything you need, Billy, before we go?"

"I'll be comfy," said Billy.

"I wish you could go with us," said Suzanne.

"I've done my share of mountain climbing," said Billy. "Just get back before dark."

"You're beginning to sound like a father," said Mouse, grinning at him.

"I wasn't worried about you," Billy told her. "I was worried about me. Reading about this bogeyman when I'm all alone in a cabin could get a little scary."

"How far have you gotten?" Mouse asked him.

"About halfway through."

"It gets even scarier."

"Come on, let's go," said Suzanne. "I'm ready for a good hike."

Two reluctant kids followed her out the door.

MOUSE HAD HAD HOPES of the hike being too much for her mother, of her mom conking out at some point and leaving them alone in the woods. No such luck. Her mom appeared to be in much better shape than either of them and they were in danger of being left behind.

"Hey, can't you slow it down?" Mouse finally called out, watching her mom climb almost straight up without even pausing to catch her breath. Well, she had run in the marathon, but she didn't see how that made her mother a good climber.

"She really moves, doesn't she," said Daryl, as winded as Mouse was.

"Well, I guess we might as well wear ourselves out," said Mouse. "It's for sure I'll be going to bed early."

"And alone," said Daryl with a chuckle.

"Laugh. You're going to be alone, too."

"Hey, it's only one night. Anyway, I like Billy."

"I like my mom, too. I guess I ought to spend a little more time with her, I won't be seeing her again before Christmas."

"Where's she going after she lets you off? She going back to the city?"

"She's going to find her place in the sun."

"What's that supposed to mean?"

"I don't know exactly, Daryl. She's tired of the city, though, and wants to find a place that suits her. She figures it'll be out west somewhere."

"How's she going to work out west?"

"She doesn't have to work if she doesn't want to. She made a mint working on that soap and invested most of it in real estate."

"Hey, does that mean I'm in love with an heiress?"

"You've seen Mom. Does it look like she's going to die in the near future? Look at her; she's half a mile ahead of us already and I'm about ready to drop."

"Come on, get a move on it, we can't let your old lady show us up."

"In case you haven't noticed, she already has."

THIS WAS EXACTLY what Suzanne needed. She was definitely getting out of shape sitting in a car all day, and the exercycle wasn't enough. What she needed was to wear herself out. She hadn't slept very well last night, and she knew why, and wearing herself out might help.

That and having Billy share a room with Daryl. That was a super plan and she wished she had thought of it the night before. Because if she had, then she might not have been in Billy's room with him and they might not have kissed and she now wouldn't be confused about the thoughts she was starting to have about him. She had actually caught herself looking at *him* in the car today.

She wasn't fooling herself into thinking this was some budding romance. Any reasonable man probably would have had the same effect on her. She was human, after all. She had natural urges even though she had become adept at stifling them. And she and Billy had been thrown together a lot.

It wasn't that she didn't find him appealing. He was that, and more. There was something very sweet and unworldly about Billy that appealed to her, something not found in any of the men she had met in New York. The problem was, she was no longer the sweet, unworldly girl she had been back in Minnesota. She was older than him, probably more experienced, and certainly more cynical.

She wouldn't be doing Billy any favors by encouraging him. What Billy needed was a sweet young wife and maybe a few kids. What Billy didn't need was a former soap-opera star from the big city.

She had enjoyed kissing him, though, more than she thought she would or she wouldn't have done it. And it wasn't any good saying that Billy wasn't in any condition for anything more than kissing, because that just wasn't true. He wasn't in any condition to attack her, of course, but he wasn't the type to do that anyway. He could, however, easily be attacked. And she'd never forgive herself if she attacked that sweet cowboy; it would be taking advantage of him and she'd hate herself for it later.

She looked around and down and saw that Daryl and Mouse were like little specks, they were so far behind her. She had an urge to leave them even farther behind, to race up the side of the mountain, but the sky was getting overcast and the temperature was dropping and for all she knew she might be caught in a blizzard and never make it back.

She stopped and looked out across the mountains. It was so beautiful it didn't even look real. She felt like she was in the middle of a painting by a very good artist. She could see now why so many artists painted mountain scenes. They were so gorgeous to look at, even if the paintings did turn out to be so pretty they were boring to look at.

She better turn around. She'd ask the manager if there was a general store nearby, and if there was, she'd cook them all dinner. Maybe some soup and toasted cheese sandwiches, and later they could drink hot chocolate with marshmallows in it. It was kind of fun to have a winter day in August.

They'd make a real party of it. After all, it would probably be the last time the four of them would be together.

"THIS IS GOING TO BE FUN," said Suzanne, dumping the picture puzzle on the floor.

"I hate puzzles," said Mouse.

"This is a wonderful one, it's a picture of the mountains."

She heard Mouse groan. Then, "Mom, would you mind if Daryl and me went to my room and watched TV?"

Suzanne looked around. "These cabins don't have TVs."

"I don't believe it," said Mouse, getting up and looking around the room.

"There's probably one in the lobby," said Billy.

"I like puzzles," said Daryl, sitting on the floor beside Suzanne and helping her turn the pieces over.

"I feel like an orphan up here," said Billy, eyeing them from his bed across the room.

Daryl jumped up and said, "I'll help you down here, if you think you'll be comfortable."

"Mouse, you can make some hot chocolate," said Suzanne, and Mouse perked up a little.

"Okay, you guys, you're in for a treat," said Mouse. "I make baaaad cocoa, twice as much chocolate and choked with marshmallows."

Suzanne shuddered, too late remembering Mouse's idea of hot chocolate. It tasted rather like a candy bar.

Billy was now beside her, his left leg forming what would be the left border of the puzzle. Suzanne started to set aside all the pieces with straight edges, and Billy followed suit. Daryl, more impatient, was already trying to fit pieces together. Suzanne didn't even know why she liked puzzles. She had never yet completed one, but she kept thinking the next one would be the one. And mountains couldn't be very difficult. Mouse, knowing how she liked puzzles, usually got her one for Christmas, but it was always some abstract thing that was impossible to figure out.

"Just think," said Billy, "if I hadn't hooked up with you guys, I'd probably be sitting in a motel room all alone right now with nothing to do."

"Is that sarcasm?" asked Suzanne.

"Cowboys aren't sarcastic," said Billy. "We leave that to the city slickers."

They had part of the border already together when Suzanne saw Mouse walking toward them balancing the four mugs of cocoa. She was watching the cocoa, trying not to slop it over the edges of the mugs, and not watching where she was going, and Suzanne saw her just about to step on Billy's leg. "Watch out!" she yelled at Mouse, and Mouse, in a panic, looked down at Billy's leg, managed to avoid stepping on it, but the contents of the four mugs of cocoa went flying all over the pieces of puzzle. It was a sorry mess.

"Oh, Billy, I'm sorry, I almost stepped on you," said Mouse, squatting down beside him as though to comfort him over the near miss.

"Made a mess of the puzzle, though," said Daryl.

"Better the puzzle than Billy's leg," said Suzanne, going to the kitchen and bringing back a sponge and some paper towels.

"Well, there goes our entertainment for tonight," said Billy, picking up some of the soggy pieces that no longer bore much resemblance to a puzzle. The picture part was peeling off the back and the edges were curling up.

"I'm sorry, Mom, I'll go get another," said Mouse. "Daryl will drive me, won't you, Daryl?"

"The store's probably closed by now," said Suzanne.

"Let them try," said Billy. "I was just starting to get interested in this."

Mouse and Daryl seemed so intent on going that Suzanne said, "Sure, go ahead. Maybe you'll find a game there we could play."

Mouse and Daryl were out the door in two seconds.

"DID YOU DO THAT on purpose?" asked Daryl.

"No, of course not," said Mouse, maybe protesting a little too much, but it had been an accident. "I wouldn't hurt Billy for anything."

"Yeah, but you didn't hurt Billy, and you got rid of that puzzle in short order."

"Yes, and I'm going to get another one."

"Oh, I thought you just wanted to be alone with me for a few minutes."

Mouse moved over beside him in the truck. "Well, maybe subconsciously, but honestly, I didn't plan it."

"We'll get your mom a couple of puzzles, make her happy."

"We don't have to hurry, though."

"No, we can take our time."

"We've got all night, right?"

"Right," said Daryl, his arm going around her.

BILLY THOUGHT MAYBE that was the last they'd see of Daryl and Mouse for a while.

Suzanne was cleaning up the last of the mess, putting the wet pieces of puzzle back in the box they came in and washing the hot chocolate out of the rug. Luckily the rug was shades of brown and it blended right in.

"I made a rug like this once," said Billy.

"Right."

"I did. It's just a rag rug, fairly simple to make. Haven't you ever made a rug, Suzanne?"

"In New York you can buy rugs."

"Well, hell, you can buy rugs in Wyoming, too, but where's your pride of possession then?" And he was just arguing now for the sake of arguing because that was the only rug he had ever made and he hadn't felt all that proud of it because it had come out lopsided.

"Don't start in on the country boy, Billy."

"But I am a country boy."

"Sure, except your father owns the radio station and is a local celebrity."

"We're talking about a very small town."

"Not all that small if it has two video stores."

Billy made a calculated move. He tried to shift his leg, letting out a groan in the process and knowing that Suzanne was going to come right over and see what was the matter with him.

"Are you all right?" she asked, kneeling down beside him.

"My leg's a little stiff; I guess I ought to do those exercises."

"Well, let's get you back on the bed and I'll help you."

She pulled him up onto his good foot with both hands, but instead of letting her put her arm around his waist and lead him over to the bed, he wrapped his arms around her. Which was a risk because if she pushed him away he was a goner.

"You're biting off more than you can chew, Billy," she said, but she hadn't pushed him away yet.

"Come on, Suzanne, relax and put those arms of yours around me. A little show of affection isn't going to turn you into a pillar of salt."

She chuckled. "I wasn't worried about being turned into a pillar of salt, Billy; I was worried about what your next move would be."

"There aren't a hell of a lot of moves I'm able to make."

"There's nothing wrong with your hands."

"Is that an invitation?"

"Just an observation." But her arms went around him then, surprising him a little.

He waited for her to make a joke, some sarcastic remark, and when she didn't, he pulled her closer. He looked at her. She already had her head tilted, so he moved his lips in the general direction of hers, and hers seemed to be moving, too, and the next thing was that they were kissing and he didn't know how long he was going to be able to stand on one leg, but he was going to make sure it was as long as possible because kissing her was even better than riding a horse. Kissing her might possibly be the best thing he could ever remember doing.

When they came up for air she still didn't push him away. She laid her cheek against his chest and hugged him close and he was cursing the fact that the one time he got to hug her she was wearing so many layers of clothes he felt like he was hugging a down comforter rather than a body.

He was finally the one who had to say, "I guess I better move over to the bed. I'm getting a muscle spasm in my right leg."

She helped him over to the bed, saying, "This isn't smart of us, Billy."

"I thought it was brilliant."

"It's not going to lead to anything."

"Why does it have to lead to something? Why can't we just enjoy it for what it is?"

"Can you do that?"

"Hell, yes!" So it was a lie; so what? He'd worry about that later.

She sat down on the edge of the bed and raised a tentative hand to his hair. She was smoothing it back, and Billy knew it was springing right back. He knew that because it was an impossibility to smooth his hair down.

He reached for a handful of her hair, feeling its softness. It was as soft as a kitten's fur, maybe even softer. He wrapped a couple of strands around his fingers, then pulled her head down to his. He could feel her quick breaths on his face and he knew she was as excited as he was and he wondered when things had changed, when she had started to want him the way he wanted her.

"This is crazy, Billy," she murmured, but he didn't think it was crazy at all. In fact he thought it eminently sane that two adults should feel like this about each other.

He reached a tentative hand out and lightly traced the outline of her breast beneath the layers of clothes. He saw a shiver go through her as he teased her breast, hardly believing that he was touching what he had been furtively trying to catch a glimpse of all week. He wanted to see them. Just once he wanted to see more than the whites of the sides. "I want to see them," he thought, "I want to see them," but he had spoken it aloud, he saw the knowledge of that in her eyes.

They widened slightly and her lips parted and there was a flush to her cheeks. She hesitated only a moment, and then she reached down and lifted up the layers of sweatshirts, not slowly, not in a teasing way, just lifted them up and let him see them.

He saw that they stood out creamy white against her tanned skin, not as small as he'd thought, but rounded and turned up at the ends, the nipples pink and protruding. And then his mouth was going to one of them and she let go of the sweatshirts and grabbed his head and the material was coming down over his forehead, and he was tasting her and making her moan while she pressed his head in harder and harder against her.

Billy was thinking to himself that he hoped the kids got lost in the woods. But as soon as he thought that, damned if he didn't hear a truck pull up outside as though his thought had conjured it up.

He wasn't sure Suzanne had heard it because she didn't even move. He drew his mouth away from her breast and pulled her clothes back down. She was trembling, not moving, just trembling, and he said, "Better get a move on, that's the kids."

Suzanne put a hand up to her chest as though to still whatever she was feeling there. He had to put his hands on her shoulders and shake her a little. "Go on now, pretend you were helping me with my exercises."

Suzanne slowly stood up, but she didn't seem capable of doing anything but staring down at him with longing. "Hey, tomorrow night we'll be all alone," he told her.

She smiled, shook her head a little and was moving away from the bed when the door opened and the kids came in.

"We got the same puzzle, Mom, and another one," said Mouse, and Billy saw that Daryl had a six-pack of beer in one hand. Hell, he could use a beer. They could probably all use a beer.

He almost laughed out loud at the sight of the four of them. They all looked a little rumpled; Mouse's cheeks were flushed as pink as her mothers, although in her case it could have been the cold. They all looked a little bit guilty and he was sure every one of them would rather be doing something else.

But instead they'd be doing a picture puzzle. Sometimes life just didn't make sense.

Chapter Nine

The University of Colorado campus summoned up some urge in Suzanne she hadn't known existed.

There had been universities in New York, quite good ones; academically better than what she was seeing now. But they had never spoken to her the way this one was. She wanted to shop in the bookstore, have coffee in the student union; she wanted to browse in the library; she wanted to sit under a tree and write in a notebook; she wanted to sit in on classes and listen to the professors; she wanted to learn everything there was to learn.

In short, she knew what she wanted to do with her life. She wanted to go back to school.

"Mom, let's just go see my dorm," said Mouse for about the fifth time. They had left Daryl and a worn-out Billy in the student union and were now wandering around on their own.

"Don't you love it, Mouse? Isn't it great? I've always loved college campuses like this. I suppose it's partly because I grew up in a college town."

"It's all right," said Mouse.

"All right? Aren't you even excited?"

"Mom, it's just another school. Maybe there's skiing and maybe the scenery's pretty, but it's still just a school, which means studying."

"But studying what you want. Learning to be something. It won't be anything like high school, Mouse, I promise."

"Well, why don't you stay and I'll do something else."

"Don't think I wouldn't like to. In fact, if you weren't going here, I would. I imagine you'd be embarrassed, though, to have your mother at the same college."

"You can knock off the sales pitch, Mom; I haven't dropped out of school yet."

Suzanne tried to control her enthusiasm. She knew how it was. If your parents raved about college educations that was about the last thing you wanted. Conversely, if she had told Mouse she thought sending her to college was a waste of money, Mouse would have been begging to go.

Anyway, it was too late to get in even if she wanted to, which she didn't. Not Colorado, anyway. There'd never be time to get her transcripts from Minnesota. She'd find her own college, though. A peaceful-looking campus like this, and maybe some mountains if she could find them. She liked the mountains. But not at the same school as her daughter. She knew Mouse wouldn't want her mother hanging around, and Suzanne wasn't sure she wanted a teenage daughter hanging around, either.

"Okay, let's find your dorm," said Suzanne, eager now to get her daughter settled and thus be that much closer to finding her own place.

"YOU SURE YOU DON'T MIND us leaving today?" Suzanne asked her, hugging her close. "We can get rooms in town for the night."

"No, why don't you go on, Mom? I think the sooner you get Billy home the better." And the longer they postponed it, the harder she thought it would be for her mother to leave. She was half afraid she was ready to move in the dorm with her and share a room.

"I'm okay," said Billy.

"But we haven't even shopped for your room," said Suzanne.

"Mom, I'll do that with my roommate when she gets here. That way we can color coordinate."

"I guess I'll be moving on, too," said Daryl, which was exactly the right thing for him to say.

"I want to thank you, Daryl," said Suzanne. "It's been fun having you along and I know Mouse enjoyed your company."

Just not how much, thought Mouse.

"It's been a pleasure getting to know you folks," said Daryl, shaking hands with her mom and then Billy.

Suzanne gave Mouse one final hug. "You won't know where I'll be, honey, so I'll give you a call every few days and see how you're doing."

"Why don't we make a time, Mom, so I'm sure to be in. How about on Monday nights?"

"But that's days away. What if you need me for something?"

"Mom. I'm an adult now; I can take care of myself."

"You're right. You're absolutely right. I would have hated it if my parents had acted the way I'm acting."

It was still another twenty minutes before her mom and Billy drove off, though. When they were finally out of sight, Mouse turned to Daryl and they both burst out laughing.

"What now?" asked Daryl.

"I don't know. You feel like going to college?"

"No."

"Neither do I."

"What do you feel like doing?"

"I don't know, Daryl. What do you feel like doing?"

"Right this minute or for the rest of my life?"

"You can start with right this minute."

"I could do with a hamburger."

"We could get some and take them back to my dorm."

"You allowed to have me there?"

"I don't know. If I'm not, what can they do to me if they catch me?"

"Throw you out of school."

"Great. Let's give it a try."

BILLY GLANCED OVER AT Suzanne. She was different. There was an excitement about her, and it had nothing to do with him. He thought she'd be depressed about now, particularly after seeing how reluctant she had been to part from Mouse, and he'd had it in mind to cheer her up, but instead she had a secret little smile on her face and she seemed a million miles away.

"I figured you'd be crying along about now," said Billy, testing the waters.

"Crying? Have you ever seen me cry?"

"Now that I think about it, no. But this was the first time I saw you go through an emotional experience."

"I don't cry from guilt."

Billy sat for a moment thinking about that. The more he thought about it, the less sense it made. "You lost me somewhere, Suzanne. Where does guilt come in? Or are you thinking about letting me out on the road to hitchhike the rest of the way home?"

"Mothers are supposed to feel a deep, wrenching loss when the last of their children leaves home."

"You have *more* kids?"

"No, just Mouse. But there's supposed to be something called an empty-nest syndrome."

"Yeah. My mom had that. Didn't last long, though."

"Mine never even showed up. I feel marvelous, Billy; I feel free. I can do whatever I want for the rest of my life."

"It's not like you don't love Mouse. Hell, anyone could see how close you two are."

"Yes, but I was never one of those mothers who want to live their lives through their children. I want to live my own life. It would be nice not to live too far away from her, though."

"Not a damn thing wrong with that." Unless, of course, she wasn't planning on including him in that life, and so far all the indications were that she wasn't. He figured tonight he would give it his best shot at changing her mind.

"You know, Billy? I suddenly realized today what I want to do with my life."

Billy didn't even want to ask what that was. If she had said she had realized it last night, then maybe he would figure it had something to do with him. But today? Hell, he hadn't done a damn thing today. Oh, there'd been a little tension between them on the drive, a good kind of tension. But for some reason it seemed to have dissipated about the time they hit Boulder and it hadn't as yet come back.

"I want to go back to school," she said.

"Come again?"

"I want to finish my college education. I knew it the minute I walked on that campus. I really love learning things, Billy, and for fifteen years I haven't learned a damn thing except how to smile and use cue cards. And I used to be fairly intelligent.''

''Well, nothing's stopping you from going back to school, I guess.'' He couldn't see it himself, but what the hell? He wouldn't care if his wife went to school. Wife? Is that what he was thinking? He guessed it was—it had a pretty good ring to it.

''Nothing at all. Lots of older people are going back to school these days. And the good thing is, I'll be able to concentrate on my studies because it won't be a social life I'm going for. Or skiing.''

''You sound real excited.''

''I am. You know what, Billy? I could keep going for years if I wanted to. I could get degrees in just about everything.''

''Kind of like a hobby?''

''It sounds silly, doesn't it? I guess once I start I'll find out what I want to specialize in. Just think, I could become an authority on something.''

''It's nice to see you've found an interest in life,'' which was an outright lie but that didn't bother Billy unduly. Sometimes you had to lie; either that or knock some sense into her.

''I'll have to find exactly the right college. Somewhere nice and peaceful. No big cities, I'm tired of big cities. I wouldn't mind one with mountains; I think I've fallen in love with mountains.''

How the hell was he going to compete with the Rockies?

''Will we reach your ranch today, Billy?''

Billy, who was fairly intelligent himself, put together a few more lies. With the best intentions, of course. ''No, not today. We ought to get as far as Laramie today, though, and to my place sometime tomorrow.''

Suzanne sighed.

"Sorry you're not getting rid of me so fast. You can always put me on a bus."

She reached over and put a hand on his leg, only it was his bad leg and it made him wince. "I'm not eager to get rid of you, Billy. And no matter how excited I am, that doesn't change the facts. It's going to be too late for me to get into any school for the fall semester."

"You could always audit classes."

The excitement was back in her voice. "I could, couldn't I?"

"Let's move back to where you were saying you weren't eager to get rid of me."

"I've become very fond of you, Billy."

"Oh, no! That's your Barbara Jean voice with that phony sound to it. Fond of me? Is that what it was last night? Is that how you are with people you're fond of?"

Suzanne didn't say anything, but neither did Barbara Jean.

"You wanted me last night, Suzanne, and nothing you say now's going to change that fact."

"What if I did?"

"Well, what in hell changed your mind today?"

"Nothing."

"You're not being very articulate for a potential college student."

"I just don't want to hurt you, Billy."

"Well damn, Suzanne, there are other positions for making love, you know."

"I wasn't talking about hurting your leg. And I'm quite aware that there are other positions. And furthermore, I don't feel like discussing positions while driving, if you don't mind."

"Sorry. Okay, that was a little crude."

"Don't apologize, Billy. That was Barbara Jean coming out again. I just can't seem to get rid of her entirely."

"What're you afraid of, Suzanne? You think that making love with me is going to leave me with a broken heart?"

"Don't start coming off as a tough cowboy, Billy. I'm aware of how you feel about me."

"And I'm aware it's mutual."

"Yes, but I can walk away from it."

"The tough New Yorker, huh? Well, maybe I'm just a romantic cowboy at heart, but I'll recover. And I'd still rather make love to you and lose you than never make love at all."

"Are those the lyrics to a cowboy song?"

Billy chuckled. "Probably."

"Let's just see what develops."

"Oh, hell, Suzanne, you know damn well what's going to develop. Exactly what would have developed last night if we hadn't been interrupted. And don't even think about getting separate rooms tonight because it would end up a pure waste of money."

Suzanne started to smile.

"And if you don't put a sweatshirt back on over that top of yours, I might not wait until tonight."

"But it's not cold out."

"I could make it even warmer."

"Behave yourself, Billy. I know it's boring sitting there, but these mountain roads are scary enough without you getting me excited."

"Am I getting you excited?" His eyes went to her skirt. "You wear anything under those little skirts of yours?"

"Of course I do. What a question!"

"It's a question that's been bothering the hell out of me ever since we met." He reached over and lifted the skirt an inch, which was all it took in order for him to see a little bit of white lace.

She took her hand off the steering wheel long enough to slap his hand away. "How about singing some songs."

"That was to amuse Mouse."

"Well, amuse me this time. Either that or you're going to spend the rest of the trip sitting in the back."

"You talk real tough, lady. How come you don't have one of those little skirts in black leather?"

"Billy!"

"Okay, okay. I'll sing you my college cheer song, that ought to get you in the mood.

"For what?"

"For college, Suzanne, what else?"

THEY GOT INTO LARAMIE a little after six and Billy directed her to a hotel. She liked the looks of the place even better than Boulder. It had mountains and lots of blue sky and just the right amount of people. And the people not only looked healthy, they looked happy. It was about as different from New York as you could get.

Billy registered them at the hotel while Suzanne hung back, hoping nobody would recognize her. Once in the room, Billy said, "Let's go for a little ride."

"A ride? We've been driving for hours."

"Come on, I'll take you out to eat. There's a great steak place in Laramie. Actually, there's more than one, but I'll take you to my favorite."

"Aren't you tired? We could get room service."

"I'd like to show you around a little."

He had to be up to something. They were finally alone, and he wanted to show her around the town? This sure wasn't the same Billy who had been teasing her in the car.

She washed up a little and then they headed back to the parking lot. "What're you up to, Billy Blue?" she asked him when she was behind the wheel once again.

"I'd just like you to see Laramie, that's all."

"I couldn't see it in the morning?"

"Sure you could, but we have plenty of time now. What's the matter, you can't wait to get alone with me?"

"I wasn't the one doing the attacking in the car."

"That was just teasing. You'll know the difference when I really attack you."

"But you're not in the mood anymore."

"Hell, yes, I'm in the mood—take a right here, okay, and a left at the next light."

"I like it here."

"Laramie's okay. A little big. . . ."

"Big? There's more people living in my neighborhood in New York."

"Wait'll you see where I live. God's country. You won't find another person for miles."

"Except your twin."

"I meant neighbors. Okay, now you keep going straight here; it's not much farther."

"I thought the steak house would be right in town."

"You hungry?"

"You said you wanted to take me for steaks."

"I want to show you something first."

What the hell, why not humor him? If they were in New York she'd want to show him around, and this was Wyoming. She couldn't blame him for being proud of it, either. There was nothing not to like.

"What is this? What are all those buildings?" Then she saw the sign. "The University of Wyoming? I didn't even know it had a university."

"Hell, woman, where've you been all your life? Why, we were in the Rose Bowl last year."

"That's a big fat lie, Billy, and you know it!"

"I just wasn't sure whether you'd know it."

"I come from a Big Ten state; I know all about the Rose Bowl." She slowed down and looked around. "It's wonderful; I like it even better than where Mouse is going."

"We have better skiing, too. Not nearly as crowded."

"Thank you. Thank you for showing me, that was really nice of you."

"The thing is, if you went to college here, Mouse would be only a short flight away."

"It's not even a long drive."

"It'd be easy to see each other on holidays."

"I think I'd like to see Montana, too."

"Montana? Who ever heard of a university in Montana?"

"And, of course, you live in Wyoming."

"Well, wouldn't it be nice to know someone else in the state? I could even drive down here and take you out for a date."

"Or you could ride your horse down."

"You know what I've noticed about you, Suzanne? You get extra sarcastic when you're hungry. Make a U-turn anywhere and we'll head back to the restaurant."

Suzanne ignored him and kept driving until they had driven through the entire campus. It was perfect, truly perfect. And she wouldn't mind having Billy in the same state. Hell, why not date in college? Everyone else did.

BILLY HAD NEVER KNOWN A WOMAN who acted more natural about her body than Suzanne. Maybe it had something to do with the fact that she worked on it, kept it in shape. She didn't use it in any kind of sexy way, at least she didn't wiggle her hips or stick our her chest, but she moved with the grace of a natural athlete and he found that even sexier. That and the way she clothed herself in as little as possible. Hell, there was a time they would have arrested a woman for walking around like that.

Now here he was, propped up in the hotel bed and incapable of even removing his jeans by himself without expending so much effort he'd be too tired to do anything else the rest of the night, and she was casually taking off her top and kicking off her shoes and walking around in her socks and little skirt and looking totally at ease with herself and with him.

"You tryin' to drive me crazy, woman?" he asked her.

Suzanne paused for a moment, then grinned at him. "Is it working?"

"Come over here and find out."

Suzanne approached the bed but stayed just out of his reach. "I've never made love with a cowboy."

"Well, if you'd move just a little bit closer...."

Suzanne took a step backward.

"Your teasing's going to be the ruin of me."

"I'm not teasing you, Billy."

"Well, what in hell do you call it?"

"I'm getting ready to take a shower."

"You have to do that right now?"

Suzanne nodded. "And then, when I'm finished with my shower, I'm going to give you a sponge bath. All over that lovely body of yours."

"Hell, it ain't so lovely," said Billy, but he was pleased no end. He didn't think he'd be able to wait for her to start rubbing his body with a sponge.

Suzanne began to smile as she pulled off her skirt and was left in just white socks and a little bit of white lace. Billy thought it was a hundred times more appealing than black nightgowns or garter belts or the other stuff they posed women in in those men's magazines. He thought of asking her to leave the socks on but he was afraid it would make him sound kinky. Hell, it probably was kinky. All he knew was that from now on he'd probably get excited seeing women in socks.

"I suppose a fast shower would be all right," said Billy.

Suzanne disappeared into the bathroom for a few minutes and he heard the shower running. When she came out, she was wearing a towel and nothing else. The towel didn't look half bad, either. She was carrying the wastebasket filled with water and a washcloth.

"You need some help undressing?" she asked him.

"I guess that depends on whether you like men naked or half dressed."

"It depends on the man," she said, taking his shoes off for him. "I'd say no to cowboy boots in bed, though; they don't look all that comfortable."

"You know, of course, what this is doing to the little bit of ego I still have left."

"That's one of the things I like about you—no macho tendencies."

"Oh, I had 'em, all right, but they kind of went over that cliff with my car." Not that he'd ever been all that macho. He thought it was pretty stupid behavior. He knew his sister went for guys that were macho, but that was probably because she was so damn macho herself.

Billy undid his belt buckle and unzipped his Levi's. Then, while he lifted himself up, Suzanne carefully pulled them off.

"How's your leg feeling?"

"It'll be okay. I just took a pain pill."

"It seems a shame you have to take a pain pill to make love to me."

"I hadn't thought about it before, but I hope it doesn't deaden anything else besides my leg."

"You don't look dead to me," observed Suzanne, reaching for his boxer shorts.

"This is a little embarrassing."

"Well, we can stop if you want—"

"Oh, no; it's not that embarrassing."

By the time she got his shorts off Billy knew the pain pill wasn't interfering with anything at all, judging by the way he was feeling.

"You going to wash me all over?" he asked.

"Oh, yes."

Billy gave a sigh of pure pleasure.

Slowly, gently, but with the feel of a continuous caress, she began to rub the washcloth all over his body. It was so far removed from the way the nurses had washed him in the hospital that there should have been another word for it. Billy closed his eyes for a minute and just enjoyed it.

"I'm not putting you to sleep, am I?" she asked.

Billy opened his eyes and smiled at her. "Where were you when I was in the hospital?"

"Actually, only a few blocks away."

"What a shame."

"If someone had told me there was a poor, lonely cowboy in the hospital with no one to visit him, I would've come over."

"What would you have done when you came over?" asked Billy, then moaned with pleasure as the washcloth moved across his loins.

"I would've brought you candy."

"What else?"

"Oh, maybe some flowers."

"What else?"

Suzanne looked up from what she was doing and their eyes met. "I would've taken you home with me."

"You're a sweet liar, Suzanne."

She smiled a little sadly. "I suppose. It's too bad the chances we miss, isn't it?"

"We caught up with it."

"We did, didn't we?"

She worked a little faster then, rinsing him off, then going to the bathroom for a towel. He took it from her and began to dry himself, and as he did so, Suzanne let her towel drop to the floor and his eyes went to the damp curls between her legs. "Get on this bed, woman!"

Suzanne grinned at him. "You're going to maintain that tough image to the end, right?"

"Let me at least talk big."

Suzanne got on the bed beside him and snuggled close. "Come on, cowboy, give me a kiss."

He pulled her over half on top of him, so delighted to have her entire naked body at his disposal that he hardly knew what part of her to touch first. It was like having ten different desserts spread out before him and he knew he was in serious danger of overindulging. He couldn't help it, though; she was so damn beautiful, and if this wasn't true love then there wasn't any such thing.

He was kissing her and running his hands down her back, trying to determine which side road to turn off at first, when he felt an electric charge go through him and he jumped pretty near two inches in the air.

"Don't you like that?" she murmured, her tongue tracing the outline of his mouth.

"Just surprised me, is all. Hey, don't stop; I promise I won't jump again."

"You cowboys all built this well?"

"Just shut up, woman, and forget the play-by-play."

"That was a compliment, Billy."

"Hell, I know that. It's just that I can't kiss and talk at the same time, unlike some New Yorkers I know."

One of his hands took off in an easterly direction and the other kept on heading due south. When it arrived it was just the way he'd always heard the south was: hot and humid. He made a little growling noise in his throat and she answered it with a growl of her own.

"I know we should take it slow and easy, Suzanne; get to know each other and all that. But I'll be doggoned if I can wait that long."

She started to climb on top of him, being careful not to touch his leg. "I'm glad you said that because I didn't want you accusing me of being a fast New Yorker, but the suspense was killing me."

With her knees on either side of him and her long, moonlight hair swinging over his face, she lifted up for a brief moment, then slowly came down, enfolding him in her body with a circular motion, the likes of which he had never experienced and which he hoped he'd get to experience a whole lot more times because it was exactly like he always imagined being electrocuted would feel like only the major difference was he wanted to keep getting electrocuted forever and ever.

He yelled out a few incomprehensible things that made absolutely no sense at all and she answered with a few of her own, which made it all right because they were on the same wavelength.

She was moving with a fluid motion not unlike the way people from the East rode horses, and he wanted so much to move with her, to meet her every move, and it was almost worth risking having to go back in the hospital over, but when he tried a move of his own, she leaned down and spoke in his mouth, "No, Billy, I don't want to hurt you," and then her mouth was closing over his and they were breathing the same air and occupying the same space and, faster than he would have liked, crying out at the same time.

And then all motion slowed down and at exactly the right moment stopped completely, and she was coming to rest on his chest and he was hanging on to her and telling her he loved her and about crying with joy all at the same time.

He made himself count to ten before speaking, but then he couldn't hold it in any longer. "Are we perfect together or am I dreaming?"

"We're perfect," she said, running her lips over his neck.

"I feel like we invented sex. Like there was never any such thing before but we had to invent it in order to do physically what was already in our minds."

"Are those the lyrics to some cowboy song?"

"You're sarcastic after sex, too?"

She lifted her head and looked down at him, her eyes laughing. "I think you should be the one on the radio. You're poetic, Billy, you know that?"

"I'm just trying to put into words what I feel."

"You know what I'm thinking?"

"Tell me."

"I'm wondering what I thought I was accomplishing all those years being celibate."

"You were waiting for me."

"I think you're right. This is true love, isn't it?"

"As true as it's ever going to be. And just to prove it, darlin', how about marrying me?"

"I'm not looking to get married, Billy."

"That's okay, then how about moving in with me for the rest of your life?"

Suzanne took his hand and brought it up to her face, leaning her cheek against it. "Let's not rush this, Billy."

"Hell, no, I figure to give you the entire weekend to think about it."

"Isn't it enough to just be in love?"

"I guess I'm a little greedy. Now that I love you, I don't want to let you out of my sight."

"I've never lived alone, Billy, not even for a day. I've never been completely on my own."

"Is that important to you?"

"I think so."

"Well, quit sounding so serious. I'm not about to lasso you to the ground and brand you. I guess I just want to know you won't disappear."

"I won't."

"That a promise?"

She moved his hand to her breast, saying, "Cross my heart."

"That's good enough for me," said Billy.

Chapter Ten

Suzanne slowed down to the legal speed limit as she drove through the small town. It was like a smaller version of Laramie and just as charming.

"This is Marathon," said Billy, waving to someone in a truck that passed them going in the other direction.

"Marathon?"

"Where my folks live. And my brother. I don't think I've told you about my brother."

"Wait a minute, Billy, and never mind your brother. This is where you *live*?"

"Not in town, no. Our ranch is a few miles further."

"But this is only an hour from Laramie."

"Right. Just a hop, skip and jump when you feel the need for a big city."

"But you said we couldn't make it here yesterday. You said we'd need to spend the night in a hotel."

"You didn't enjoy last night?"

"That's not the point, Billy. You lied to me."

"Sure I did. I've been lying to you every once in a while ever since I met you."

"But why? We could've been at your ranch last night."

"I wanted you all to myself just for one night, Suzanne. I kind of wanted to consolidate our relationship before taking you home."

"I can't believe we're here already. I thought we'd be driving all day."

"Isn't that a nice surprise?"

"You could've told me. I wouldn't have said no to staying in a hotel last night."

"I wasn't taking any chances. So, how do you like Marathon?"

"Fine, what I saw of it."

"It's small, but it's got everything a person could need."

"Don't you think you should have warned your sister we'd be arriving today?"

"Already did. I called her this morning while you were in the shower."

"What'd she say?"

"What you got to understand about Wendy is that she's not used to me bringing women home."

"What did she say?"

"We're both, I guess, kind of set in our ways."

"Tell me what she said before I punch you, Billy."

"Well, she knew you were driving me home; hell, I told her about that clear back in Ohio."

"You sound like you're afraid of her."

"Afraid of my own sister?"

"So what did she say?"

"Well, I kind of hinted that we'd become more than friends on the road."

"You kind of hinted?"

"I told her we were in love."

She looked over at Billy. His hands were clenched, the knuckles showing white. He was under stress, no doubt about it, and it must be related to his sister. "Was she happy for you, Billy?"

"I have no idea."

"Well, what did she say?"

"Nothing. She hung up on me."

"Did you call her back?"

"No use calling Wendy back when she's in one of her tempers. She'd just rip the phone out of the wall."

Suzanne thought Billy was worrying unnecessarily. She knew she'd get along with his sister; she always got along with women. All her life she had had close female friends, all with different backgrounds—take Jaime, Abbie and Marielle. Besides, if Wendy was anything like Billy—and as his twin she was pretty sure she would be— then she didn't know why they wouldn't get along fine.

Of course it would be a shock hearing your brother had fallen in love with some strange woman whose daughter had knocked his car off a cliff. That sounded a little suspect. Maybe Wendy thought she was after Billy's ranch, intent on displacing his sister. Well, Suzanne would put her straight on that soon enough. She wasn't after the ranch and she wasn't after Billy. She might love him, but she didn't want to own him. As far as that went, she didn't even want to live with him. She'd never lived alone for even one day in her entire life and she was looking forward to the experience.

"See out there? See that tree?" asked Billy. They had already passed the tree, but Suzanne turned around to see it. It looked ordinary enough. Maybe in New York she would have looked twice at it, but here it was nothing special. "What about it?"

"That tree's the start of our property."

"We're there, then?" asked Suzanne, not seeing any signs of a house.

"Not yet. Not for a few more miles."

"You own all of this?"

"I know it doesn't look like much; mostly it's just grazing land for the cattle."

"Listen, I'm impressed. All I own is fifteen hundred square feet. And in New York that seemed like a lot."

"You talking about your apartment?"

Suzanne nodded.

"Hell, we give our pigs more room than that."

"How big's your house?"

"Not all that big. Comfortable, though."

Suzanne speeded up. There wasn't any other traffic on the road and she was getting eager to see his place. And Wendy. She wanted to put the woman's mind at ease right away and make things less stressful for Billy. He'd invited her to stay over the weekend, and she had agreed, but not if things were going to be difficult for him.

Actually he'd invited her to stay forever, but she told him it was a little too soon to think about that. She hadn't told him it was too soon by several years, but she had been thinking it. He had marriage on his mind and she didn't even want to think about that. Marriage was what had ended her college days the last time; she wasn't going to let it happen again.

Not that she wasn't just as tempted with Billy as she had been with Sweet Basil, and for the same reasons. She had felt rushed with Sweet Basil, though. He had been leaving for New York and if she hadn't gone with him it would all have been over. There was no rush with Billy; Billy wasn't going anywhere.

A building came into view on the right but it looked more like a motel than a house. It was rustic and in need of paint and there were no trees or shrubs to soften the look of the building. She saw a couple of lawn chairs on the long veranda and a barbecue. "Is this it?" asked Suzanne.

"No, that's where the guys stay. I guess you'd call them the real cowboys."

"You have ranch hands?"

"Of course we do. It's too much for two people to manage, although Wendy and I did it the first couple of years with a little help from some friends."

At the next bend the house came into view. It was an A-frame, all wood and glass, and she could see the mountains and sky reflected in the large expanse of glass. A porch with a wooden railing stretched across the front and she counted a half dozen redwood chairs. There were some shrubs and flowers around the house but they didn't look planned; they looked like they were growing wild.

"Home sweet home," said Billy.

"Maybe I ought to just drop you off."

"You chickening out, Suzanne?"

"You sure you have room for me?"

"Wendy and I have separate rooms, and I figure you can share mine."

"You just have two bedrooms?"

"We figured that was all we needed."

There was no lawn and no discernible driveway, so Suzanne just pulled up in front of the house and parked. She got out and went around to open the door for Billy, but he was already getting out. She reached into the back for his crutches and handed them to him.

"How does it feel to be home?"

"There were times I didn't think I'd make it."

"It doesn't look as though anyone is around."

"Oh, Wendy's around. Probably watching us from a distance."

Suzanne could see for miles and there was no sign of a woman on a horse. She decided to leave her bags in the car for now just in case she wanted to make a fast getaway.

Billy needed help climbing the four steps, then he was across the porch and sliding open the unlocked screen door. He held it for Suzanne and she walked inside.

It was an enormous room and filled with sunlight. A balcony ran across the back with access by a steep set of stairs. She could see two rooms up there and assumed they were the bedrooms.

"How're you going to manage those stairs?" she asked Billy.

"With great difficulty. I might have to sleep down here until I'm on a cane."

The walls and floors were all natural wood, which gave the place a feeling of warmth. There was a big fireplace made out of stone with stacks of logs piled up on either side of it. It looked well used. "Is that the only heat you have?" she asked him.

"Just about. Wendy and I have electric heaters in the bedrooms, but that fireplace really keeps the place warm. We also have a wood-burning stove in the kitchen."

There was an enormous sectional covered in brown corduroy facing the fireplace with pillows of different colors piled up on it haphazardly. The coffee table looked like a big block of wood and had newspapers and magazines and a couple of dirty mugs. Suzanne didn't recognize any of the magazines. On the floor was a well-worn Oriental rug.

The room was so large she almost didn't notice the grand piano practically lost in one corner with some sheet music set out. In another corner she saw a loom, but it looked more decorative than functional. One wall was bookshelves and the books were all paperback.

"Who plays the piano?"

"We both do. Mom was big on piano lessons. We weren't, though, so about all we can play is 'Chopsticks' as a duet with a few of our own variations."

"And the loom?"

"We tried. When we first started ranching Wendy and I had this idea we wanted to be entirely self-sufficient. We were going to build all our furniture and make all our clothes. That notion didn't last long. We seem to have a talent for ranching, but neither of us can even assemble furniture let alone do something as difficult as sewing. I did make a rug, though, I wasn't kidding about that. It's in my room."

Behind the living room was another large room, this one the kitchen. It had a table big enough to seat a dozen with benches along the sides and the windows had a stunning view of the mountains. The appliances were modern and a Mr. Coffee machine sat on one of the counters. There were dirty dishes in the sink and a frying pan on the stove had traces of egg in it.

"So, you like my place?"

"In New York, they'd cut up a space like this and make six studio apartments."

"What do you think of it?"

"It's great. No locks on the doors, nothing covering the windows. It would take some getting used to."

"Locking doors would take some getting used to for me. You know you locked up your jeep outside?"

"Habit."

Billy went over to a wall phone, leaned one of his crutches against the wall and started to punch out some numbers. "I'm going to give Wendy a buzz, tell her we're here."

"You're calling her on the phone?"

"She's got a phone in the Jeep." He propped himself upright against the wall. "Yeah, we're here," she heard him say, then he didn't say anything else until he hung up. "Tried to give me some story about how they're having a problem with a calf, but I told her to get in here. It's nothing the guys can't handle."

He moved around the kitchen on one crutch, grabbing on to the counters for support. He got the Mr. Coffee machine going, then turned to her and said, "I forgot, you only drink coffee in the morning." He opened the refrigerator and surveyed the contents. "No Coke, but there's some iced tea. You drink iced tea?"

"Sure," said Suzanne, feeling somehow out of place. In the car she had been in charge, but in his own house he had naturally taken over and she began to feel like a third crutch.

"Don't worry about Wendy," he said.

"I wasn't worried; should I be?"

"I don't know what kind of reaction I'm going to get. I never brought anyone home before."

"What are you guys running here, a monastery?"

He grinned a little foolishly. "Wendy goes out; sometimes doesn't come home for days. I went out, too, but not as much as Wendy. We just never tried moving anyone in here."

"I have no intention of moving in," said Suzanne. "You invited me for the weekend, but if it's going to be a problem, I'll go back to Laramie and get a room."

"Yeah, I'll explain you're a weekend guest. The thing is, Wendy's going to sense something."

"What's there to sense?"

"You know what I'm talking about. We're real close. She probably knows more about me than anyone in the world."

"I'm bound to like her, Billy, if she's your twin."

"We're not identical—"

"I *know* that. It's not biologically possible."

"I'm more easygoing than she is."

"Billy, if you're trying to tell me your sister's a bitch—"

"No, she just has a temper, that's all."

"Look, Billy, no cowgirl is likely to intimidate me, so why don't you sit down and relax."

He was just about to when they both heard a car being driven up and Billy, grabbing both crutches, said, "Stay here a minute, okay? Let me talk to her alone first."

Suzanne began to feel like some scarlet woman being hidden away from the puritans. She got up and walked over to the door leading into the living room. She had a good view of his sister outside and could hear each word that was being shouted.

"What the hell's that red toy there, Billy? Is that some kind of joke? Is that some yuppie New Yorker's idea of a four-wheel drive?"

"It's a Suzuki, Wendy—"

"Hell, I could tell it was Japanese by its size. Don't tell me you drove across the country in that pile of tin; it's lucky you even made it here."

She saw Wendy heading for the front door. Suzanne walked into the living room, thinking his sister would have to at least shut up when she saw they had a guest. Wendy more than shut up. Her jaw fell open when she got a good look at Suzanne. Suzanne was treated to a minute inspection by a pair of eyes behind glasses just like Billy's. The eyes paused briefly on the running shoes and socks, moved up to the miniskirt and tank top, then rested for a moment on the baseball cap that Suzanne had forgotten to remove.

Suzanne had done her own inspection and found that they looked almost exactly alike only Wendy's hair was shorter than Billy's and she looked a lot tougher. She suspected, though, that it was pretty hard to look tough on crutches.

"Wendy, this is Suzanne," said Billy.

Wendy stood there scowling. "You mind if I have a word alone with my brother?"

"Not at all," said Suzanne, moving back into the kitchen. She didn't try to overhear what was said, but Wendy didn't know the meaning of keeping her voice down.

"What the hell *is* that?" she was demanding of her brother. "She looks to me like an update of Minnie Mouse. You serious, Billy, or what?"

"Do I make a commentary on the guys you're seen with?"

"To my knowledge I've never been seen with a freak. I just hope to God you didn't stop in town and let anyone catch sight of her or we're going to be the laughingstock of Marathon."

"I think you're jealous."

"Of *what*?"

"Of the fact that I brought home a good-looking, intelligent woman."

"Oh, yeah, Billy, next you're going to be telling me you go for her mind."

"She happens to have a very good mind."

"Yeah, under that little skirt of hers."

"The hell with you, Wendy! Don't ask me how I am; don't ask me if I'm in any pain; and for God's sake don't break down and tell me you're glad to have me home. Just stand there and be the pain in the ass you're famous for.''

There was silence for about a minute and then Suzanne heard the car start up.

She looked into the living room and saw Billy staring after his sister.

''She has rather a big mouth, doesn't she?'' asked Suzanne, joining him at the door and seeing his sister pull off in a serious-looking Jeep about twice the size of hers.

''You should've heard her when she was a kid.''

''Is there anything you need, Billy, before I go?''

''You're not going anywhere.''

''It doesn't look as though we're going to be a congenial group. I'll stay in Laramie for the weekend; I'd like to check out the university again anyway.''

''We have plenty of room—''

''Sure, and your sister can monitor our sex life from the next room in her own sweet way.''

Billy was shaking his head and grinning. ''Doggone if I hadn't forgotten how feisty Wendy can get.'' He put an arm around Suzanne and leaned into her. ''You can take my bedroom. I don't figure I'm going to be able to manage those stairs anyway.''

''I really don't think it's a good idea.''

''I figured you New Yorkers were tougher than that.''

What the hell, she was tough, wasn't she? If she could shout down some of the characters in New York who hassled her in the streets, she could certainly stand up to some ignorant cowgirl. Hell, she'd met tougher women in Bloomingdale's.

''All right, I'll stay for the weekend. It should be interesting.''

''I'm not sure I trust that gleam in your eyes.''

"Just let me get my bags out of my yuppie toy," said Suzanne, sliding open the door.

"You heard that?"

"Are you kidding? All of Marathon probably heard that."

SUZANNE REARRANGED the sectional in the living room and fashioned a bed for Billy, then insisted he rest for a while. "Go on, you probably ought to be taking naps."

"Makes me feel like a baby."

"It's called recuperating after major surgery. I'm going to give Mouse a call and tell her where she can reach me. And after that—"

"After that you're going to crawl into bed with me."

"Not with your sister on the rampage, I'm not."

She called the number for Mouse's dorm and waited while someone checked her room to see if she was in. She had thought she'd probably have to leave a message and was a little surprised when Mouse answered the phone.

"How're you doing, honey?" she asked her.

"Mom, I thought you weren't going to call until Monday."

"Well, I'm at Billy's and I thought I'd give you his number in case you have to reach me."

"You're there already?"

"We could've gotten here yesterday. Where he lives isn't all that far from your school."

"So where are you going next?"

"We stopped in Laramie and there's a university there. I was thinking I might apply."

"I knew it."

"You knew what?"

"I knew the way you were carrying on about my school that you were thinking of going back yourself."

"Well, I like the looks of this one and I like the looks of Wyoming—"

"And you like Billy."

Suzanne didn't quite know how to answer that.

"Listen, I'm not giving you a hard time, Mom; I like him, too. He's great."

"I'm not rushing into anything—"

"Of course not. You've got all the time in the world, right? How old were you on your last birthday?"

"Old enough not to act like a kid and rush into something."

"I was just kidding you, Mom. Listen, have you met his family yet?"

"Just his sister, but if she's any indication...."

"That bad?"

"Well, if there's such a thing as a bad twin and a good twin—"

"Billy's the good one."

"Right."

"Listen, Mom, I was kind of in the middle of something. How about if I call you over the weekend?"

"Okay, but take down the number," she said, reading it slowly over the phone.

"Bye, Mom—take care."

"You too, honey. I know you're going to have fun at that school."

"I'm already having fun," said Mouse.

Suzanne had just hung up when the phone rang. "Should I get it?" she called out to Billy.

"I'll pick it up in here," he said.

Suzanne went out the back door to give him some privacy. There were some smaller buildings and behind them the ranch spread out as far as she could see. It looked like a good place to run. The air was dry and cooler than it had been in Laramie, and she thought she'd change into jeans and a sweatshirt. Not that she cared what Wendy thought about her miniskirt. Hell, the woman probably wouldn't know fashion if it rode by her on a horse.

"HEY, SUZANNE," yelled Billy, then waited for her to come into the room. "That was my daddy."

"I'll bet he was glad you're home."

"Never said. Just said he'd heard from three different people that I was seen driving through town with a woman with New York plates."

"Hadn't Wendy told him I was driving you home?"

"It appears she didn't mention it. He wanted me to bring you into town and sit in on his radio show tonight, but I told him I wasn't up to it."

"You okay?" she asked, sitting down next to him.

"It's not my leg. I'm seldom up to sitting in on Daddy's program. You ever ridden a horse for twelve straight hours? No? Well that's about as tiring as listening to Daddy argue for ten minutes. The man has a mouth on him."

"Is that who Wendy takes after?"

"Nah, Wendy doesn't like to argue. Wendy's just bossy."

"What's your mom like? And that brother you mentioned briefly before."

"Generally speaking Mom's quiet and peaceful unless she catches you setting traps for animals or hunting out of season. And even in season she's not crazy about hunters. Just don't ever wear a fur coat in front of Mom."

"And your brother?"

"Mike? He's the normal one in the family. He's six years younger than me and Wendy, got married while he was still in school, and he and Janie have three kids. He's got a law office in Laramie. I'll try to round up the whole family and we'll have a barbecue tomorrow."

"Wendy might not like that."

"Then Wendy can cut out. She usually does on weekends anyway. I think she's been seeing some guy for a while but she's real closemouthed about him."

"What about lunch, Billy? You want me to fix us something?"

"Plenty of steak and eggs in the refrigerator. And after lunch we can take a nap."

"You cowboys have one-track minds."

"Yeah, don't you just love us?"

Chapter Eleven

Wendy had come home the night before but it had been late. Billy was already asleep downstairs and Suzanne was tossing and turning in his bed, trying to get comfortable on a mattress that sank so low in the middle it resembled a canyon. No matter what position she got into, she ended up rolling into the center of the bed and being enveloped by the sides of the mattress.

She heard the Jeep pull up, the car door slam and then the sliding door being opened none too gently. Then a light was turned on.

She heard Billy say, "Turn that off, will you? I'm trying to sleep."

"I have to see where I'm going, don't I?"

"Damn it, Wendy, quit bugging me."

"Where's blondie?"

If Billy replied to that, Suzanne couldn't hear him. What she could hear was some stomping around, the refrigerator being opened and slammed shut and then the sound of a tab being pulled off a can. The acoustics in the house were phenomenal, which was just as well to know.

Then Billy said, "It looks to be like you already lifted a few tonight."

"I'm old enough to drink."

"You're old enough to act like an adult, too, but I don't see you doing it."

There was some pretty colorful cursing out of Wendy, ending up with, "If I wanted your advice I'd petition it."

"Whatsa matter, you can't stand me being happy?"

The sound of throaty laughter carried clearly upstairs.

"Ain't no way some city woman's going to make you happy, Billy. You're a cowboy."

"You really believe that, don't you? As far as I recall, we were both brought up in Laramie. You were never even on a horse until you were fourteen years old."

"You fixing on running out on me, Billy?"

"Hell, I'm not running anywhere on crutches, Wendy."

"You know what I'm talking about."

"I love the ranch every bit as much as you do, and you ought to know that without my having to tell you."

"And you think that delicate little thing is going to survive on a ranch?"

"I didn't have it in mind to hire her on as a ranch hand."

"This house isn't big enough for the three of us."

"Wendy, will you please relax? I invited a guest for the weekend and you're making a Cecil B. DeMille production out of it. If I didn't know you better I'd think you'd been smoking some weed. Talk about paranoia...."

"I ran into Mom tonight. She's coming over tomorrow to check her out."

"Well good, 'cause I'm planning a family barbecue for tomorrow. And I'd appreciate it if you'd behave yourself. You hear me, Wendy?"

"Hell, you don't have to tell me how to behave."

"Somebody sure as hell has to."

Suzanne heard some more clomping around, then the sound of boots coming up the wooden stairs. She pulled the covers up around her, sure that Wendy would come in her room, turn on the light and check her out. Instead, she heard Wendy go into her own room, heard the sound of her boots being dropped on the floor and then heard the sound of bedsprings giving way as Wendy got into bed.

Very soon after came the snoring.

Suzanne wondered how she was ever going to get to sleep. She didn't know how Billy put up with it. If she had to sleep next door to someone who snored at that pitch she'd be tempted to go over there with a pillow and snuff out the snorer.

Suzanne counted slowly to a thousand, then got out of bed and went downstairs. When she crawled in beside Billy, he said, "Suzanne?"

"Who'd you think it was?"

"Hell, I wouldn't put it past Wendy to come down and bug me some more. Did you hear us down here?"

"Very clearly."

"Well, move over here. You don't have to leave that much room between us."

Suzanne moved closer and Billy put an arm around her. She felt like putting her arms around him and protecting him from his sister.

"How could you stand living with her all these years?"

Billy chuckled. "You gonna save me from her?"

"You ought to save yourself before it's too late. A woman like that could devour you."

"We get along fine most of the time. I think you're getting the wrong impression of me, darlin'. You see me as this poor helpless cowboy, but I've been standing up against my sister for years. And most of the time she backs down."

"I know the helpless part is a recent thing, but I see you as too nice to be a cowboy. I can't see you shooting a snake or getting into barroom fights or firing at cattle rustlers."

"You have a romanticized version of cowboys in that pretty head of yours, Suzanne. I can shoot a snake if I have to, but most of the time you don't have to worry about them. As for barroom brawls, I leave that to my father. And we haven't had any cattle rustlers in my lifetime."

"You sure you can even ride a horse?"

Billy laughed out loud. "I sure as hell didn't hurt my knee playing tennis."

Suzanne realized her back had stopped hurting. "How do you stand that bed of yours?"

"I just roll into the middle and go to sleep."

"You know, I think you need taking care of."

"You going to take care of me?"

"Is that what you want?"

"Nope. Like you, Suzanne, I want to be independent. But I'd sure as hell like you by my side."

"I am by your side."

"Don't think I hadn't noticed."

"And your sister is right above us."

Billy pulled her close so that her head rested on his shoulder. "Well, at least it's better than sharing that cabin with Daryl."

BILLY'S FATHER SHOWED up early. Boswell Blue looked like a short, portly Elvis Presley with gray sideburns. His satin cowboy shirt was just a shade short of being shocking pink and his silver cowboy boots had three-inch heels on them.

Billy answered the door and Suzanne watched Boswell giving Billy a big hug, welcoming him home. Then he turned to Suzanne, and without missing a beat, said, "Well, it's Barbara Jean. Howdy, ma'am."

"You know who she is?" asked Billy.

"I'm a media animal, Billy, it's my job to know." He was heading for Suzanne as he said this, his smile showing layers of teeth, and before Suzanne could get over her initial surprise, she was enfolded in a bear hug.

"Her name's Suzanne," said Billy.

"Just call me Bos, honey," said Billy's father, letting go of her and standing back to give her a good looking over.

Suzanne was glad she was wearing jeans and a sweatshirt as Bos's eyes weren't missing a thing.

"So this is the lady my daughter's in an uproar over."

"Wendy didn't give her a chance, Dad."

"Well, I'd surely like the opportunity to interview you on my show while you're in town. It's not often we get a celebrity in these parts."

Suzanne looked to Billy for help but Billy was grinning and keeping his mouth shut.

"I understand your shows are somewhat controversial," said Suzanne.

"Somewhat controversial? Is that what Billy told you?"

Suzanne looked at Billy again and, sensing no help was going to come from him, said, "That was the impression I got."

"They're not *some*what controversial, young lady, they're incendiary, if I do say so myself."

"I doubt whether I'd add anything to your show."

"Now that's where you're wrong, Barbara Jean. Maybe you haven't been watching your show lately, but there's a rumor spreading that Victor up and killed you and buried your body somewhere. There's a seven-state search going on for you right this moment."

"I don't think the producers would appreciate it if I showed up on your radio show and said I was alive and well in Wyoming."

"No, I'd want to question you about some of the inside stuff. You know—network gossip."

Billy finally joined in. "I was showing Suzanne over the campus when we came through Laramie. She's thinking of going back to school."

"Then you're not going back to *Reach for the Sky*?"

"No, I'm out of it," said Suzanne. "I just wish I could get into school this semester, but I didn't make up my mind until the other day."

Bos's smile had something of the con man about it. "Well, I think something could be arranged."

Suzanne looked at Billy, who said, "Dad is pretty friendly with the head of the communications department at U.W."

"I doubt whether I'd be interested in communications," said Suzanne, who had had enough of communications in the past fifteen years to last her the rest of her life. Once she started giving it some thought she had been thinking more along the lines of geology or engineering.

"The thing is," said Bos, "it's too late for you to get into the undergraduate program, but if you'd be willing to teach a class in TV, something might be arranged. And you'd get your tuition free. You'd be a natural, Barbara Jean."

"Yeah, Barbara Jean," said Billy.

"I've never taught anything," said Suzanne.

Bos, sensing victory, said, "Well, hell, they'll provide you with a textbook."

"I'll think about it," said Suzanne, which was her standard answer to Mouse's bright ideas. Although if it meant she could start school and not have to wait six months, it wouldn't be so bad. Just as long as they didn't make a big production out of her being Barbara Jean at the school. She'd rather get a little respect from her teachers.

Bos, who obviously thought everything was decided, switched to talk of Billy's knee operation. "I found you a physical therapist, son, over in Laramie, but he don't make house calls."

"I can drive," said Billy.

"That's not the way I hear it," said Bos. "The story is you had a little accident and lost your car."

"Yeah, but I wasn't in it at the time," said Billy, and she silently thanked him for not dragging her into that.

Suzanne heard a car pull up outside and looked out. She saw a long, white convertible that Bos must have come in and a dusty station wagon right behind it. The doors of the station wagon opened and three little boys piled out of the back and a sweet-faced young woman and a younger, chubbier version of the twins got out of the front.

There were introductions all around and then Mike got the barbecue out for Billy and put the coals on, the children went racing off to the stables to find their Aunt Wendy and beg for pony rides, and Suzanne and Janie went into the kitchen to prepare the food.

"We were so glad to hear Billy met someone," said Janie, giving Suzanne a shy smile.

"Aren't there any available women around here?" asked Suzanne, wondering, not for the first time, why someone as appealing as Billy didn't have the women pursuing him like crazy.

"Well, yes, but most of them know Wendy, too."

"Are you saying she scares them off?"

"She's broken up more than one of his relationships. Of course Mike always says that it couldn't happen if Billy didn't let it."

"Well, I can tell you right now we didn't hit it off."

"She takes a little getting used to."

"If you want to take the time," said Suzanne.

"The kids love her. She's just not very good with women. If you ask me, she doesn't like them. I don't really think she believes she's female."

"I don't think I made a good first impression," said Suzanne. "She came in looking like Clint Eastwood and I was wearing a miniskirt—"

"You weren't!"

Suzanne nodded.

"I've been trying to get up my nerve to buy me one of those, but Mike says I'm too old."

"Billy seems to like them."

"I'll bet he does," said Janie, giving Suzanne a big wink.

Suzanne heard a roar and looked through the door to the living room in time to see a noisy bike pull up. "Is there a relative I haven't heard about?" she asked Janie.

"That's my mother-in-law, and don't go by appearances. Ginger might ride a dirt bike, but she's a real sweetheart."

A few minutes later a pretty woman with curly red hair and freckled arms came into the kitchen. She was wearing jeans and a flowered blouse, and a motorcycle helmet was dangling from one of her hands.

"I hear we have a soap-opera star visiting us," she said, then opened her arms to Suzanne.

Suzanne wasn't used to a family that hugged all the time, but she rather liked it. "A former soap-opera star," she told Ginger.

"I thought you looked familiar," said Janie, "but I didn't want to say anything."

"So tell us," said Ginger, "did Victor kill you?"

Suzanne laughed. "That will depend on the mail the network receives."

"You mean public opinion will determine the outcome?" asked Janie.

"It has a large bearing on it," said Suzanne. "They also think I'll be back, but they're wrong. But just in case I change my mind they'll leave what happened to me open to speculation for the moment."

"I hope you won't take this wrong," said Ginger, "but I never liked your character much. If you'd started talking to me in that sappy Barbara Jean voice I might have walked right back out of the kitchen."

"If you feel that strongly, how do you think I felt having to play that idiot for fifteen years?"

Ginger looked at Janie and said, "I think my Billy might have just won himself the jackpot."

WENDY HAD GONE OUT before Suzanne got up that morning and she didn't show up until Mike went off to tell her the food was ready. She showed up followed by her three nephews, who were all imitating her walk. Suzanne didn't know whether the kids knew something about Wendy she didn't know or whether little kids just didn't have good judgment.

They all ate at the long table in the kitchen and it wasn't noticeable that Wendy wasn't doing any of the talking until she finally said to her mother, "Why're you all calling her Barbara Jean?"

"Why, that's the character she plays on *Reach for the Sky*. Suzanne's an actress."

Suzanne was about to dispute that when Wendy said, "Just what we need, a two-bit soap-opera actress."

She'd still dispute the "actress" as she had no illusions about her talent, but the "two-bit" part was way off base. She was about to say so even though she hated bragging about the money she had made, but Bos saved her the trouble.

"Hardly two-bit, I'd say," he said to his daughter. "She could probably buy your ranch with her pocket money."

There was rather a lengthy silence then until Billy said, "Hey, Suzanne, you didn't tell me you were rich."

"I wouldn't say I was rich, but I was highly overpaid." She had a feeling that a couple of them would like to hear just how overpaid, but she wasn't about to enlighten them.

"Then why're you driving that poor excuse for a jeep?" asked Wendy, smiling at her own wit.

"I thought it was cute," said Suzanne, knowing this would irritate the hell out of Wendy.

And it did. "Oh, God, save me from women who buy cars because they think they're cute. She probably thinks you're cute, too," she said to Billy.

Suzanne let that one go.

"You're being rude to a guest, Wendy," said Ginger.

"I didn't invite her."

Billy grinned at Suzanne. "Instead of Bigfoot in Wyoming, we've got Bigmouth."

"Well, do I discern a little trouble on Paradise Ranch?" asked Bos, his eyes lighting up.

"Just your daughter doing her thing," said Billy.

"You going to take us riding after dinner?" one of the boys asked Wendy.

Wendy looked across the table at Suzanne and Suzanne knew exactly what was coming next. "Do you ride?" Wendy asked her, the dimple in her cheek flashing for a moment.

"Are you referring to horses?"

Wendy nodded.

"I've ridden a few times," said Suzanne, thinking of the sedate rides through Central Park when Mouse had been in her horse-crazy stage. Which was followed a year later by her boy-crazy stage.

"Maybe we could go for a ride together after dinner."

Billy said, "Leave it alone, Wendy. Next you'll be challenging her to a shoot-out at high noon."

Wendy shrugged. "I just thought she might enjoy it. I could show her around the ranch."

Suzanne, who'd rather break her neck than back out of a dare, said, "I'd enjoy a ride around the ranch."

When dinner was over, Suzanne went out on the porch with Billy and the women while the men did the cleaning up. Wendy had taken off for the stables where she was getting two horses saddled up.

"You don't have to do this," said Billy.

"Oh, yes, I do," said Suzanne.

"You ever been on a horse?"

"I took riding lessons when I was a kid and I've been on a few times since. I've never ridden Western, though."

"Let her go," said Ginger. "Your sister's not going to leave her alone until she's proved herself."

"She doesn't have to prove herself on a horse as far as I'm concerned," said Billy.

"At least she doesn't want to drag race," said Suzanne. "She'd leave my Suzuki in the dust."

"That is a cute little car," said Ginger. "I wouldn't mind having one of those. You get good mileage?"

Suzanne was about to answer when Wendy rode around the corner of the house on a black horse, leading a brown one behind her.

"That's Danny Boy you'll be riding," said Billy. "He'll give you a gentle ride."

Suzanne didn't wait around for any instructions or last-minute warnings. She went down the steps and over to Danny Boy, taking the reins from Wendy's hand. She reached up and stroked his head a couple of times and then put her foot in the stirrup and swung herself up into the saddle. She rather liked the Western saddle; at least she'd have something to hold on to if the riding got rough.

"You bring her back in one piece," Billy called out to Wendy.

"Or what?" Wendy asked, a defiant tone to her voice.

"You don't want to know," said Billy.

"I'll be okay," said Suzanne, kicking the horse and getting him moving around Wendy. She kicked him a little harder and the horse started to trot. Suzanne tried to forget about posting and just hugged the saddle. It wasn't comfortable and she'd probably have to sleep on her stomach tonight, but it wasn't all that bad.

Wendy's horse came up even with hers and they trotted along in silence. Suzanne was beginning to relax and enjoy herself. It was a beautiful day for riding and she didn't have to worry about joggers or cyclists getting in the way.

As soon as they were out of sight of the ranch house, though, Wendy's horse broke into a gallop and Suzanne's horse followed suit. At first she was apprehensive as they seemed to be flying across the land, but she soon realized that it was a lot more comfortable than trotting.

In fact it was fun, the same sensation of speed as downhill skiing without having to freeze to death in the process.

In the distance she saw a herd of cattle, so many it would be impossible to count them. They came up to them faster than she would have supposed and Wendy slowed down to a trot. Suzanne reined in her own horse as they circled the herd.

Wendy slowed down to let her catch up and when they were next to each other she said, "Are you all right?"

"I'm fine," said Suzanne, and thought she saw a hint of disappointment in Wendy's eyes.

"You want to rest for a while?"

"No, let's keep going."

Wendy took off again at a gallop and Suzanne saw that the foothills that had been in the distance before were now close and Wendy was headed for them. Suzanne had never ridden in hills, nor had she ever done any jumping, but they had already jumped over a small stream with no trouble and she was game to try the hills.

Wendy was pulling ahead of her and Suzanne, not wanting to fall behind, kicked her horse a few times but he seemed to be running as fast as he could and the distance widened.

Suzanne was thinking about how much Mouse would enjoy this when a small animal, probably a rabbit, ran in front of her horse. The horse stopped midstride and reared up, and Suzanne was in the dirt on her very sore rear end before she could say Danny Boy.

She was more embarrassed than hurt, watching Wendy in the distance to see if she'd look back and see her, and so she didn't notice for a few moments that she was now without a horse. Danny Boy, for some unknown motive of his own, had turned around and was galloping back the way they'd come.

"Great," said Suzanne, getting up and brushing off the seat of her pants. She was a little stiff, much the way she felt after running, and she did a few warm-up exercises to stretch her muscles.

She was stretching her hamstrings when Wendy rode up. "Where the hell's Danny Boy?" she asked in an accusing tone as though Suzanne had killed and buried him.

"I think he went home."

"You just let him go?"

"He threw me, okay? Something ran in front of him and he threw me off."

"I suppose I'm going to have to ride you home."

"Don't do me any favors, Wendy," said Suzanne.

Wendy, who hadn't heard her sarcasm before, was silenced for a moment. "I'm not going to have to explain to Billy that I left you out here."

"Nobody's asking you to."

Wendy circled her for a minute, looking down from the height of her horse and obviously wishing she'd disappear along with Danny Boy. "Do you think you can get up behind me by yourself?"

"Do you think you can take a flying leap?"

"Look, I brought you out here, I'll take you back."

"Go to hell, I don't need your help. I'll run back."

"You're talking about ten, eleven miles."

Suzanne looked up at her with a sweet smile, and in her most cloying Barbara Jean voice, said, "Wendy, would you mind getting out of my face?"

Wendy was still sitting there on her horse when Suzanne took off at a run in the direction they had come from. She was showing off at first, displaying a little speed for Wendy's benefit, but then she remembered she wasn't running the mile and slowed down, pacing herself. She hadn't been training lately, but then this was no twenty-six-mile marathon, either. Ten or eleven miles? A piece of cake!

She figured she had run a quarter of a mile when Wendy went by her in a flash. Then she watched as the horse turned and Wendy trotted back.

"Quit being stubborn and get up here. So you can run a few blocks, big deal!"

"Piss off, lady," said Suzanne, not even out of breath.

She figured it was the "lady" part that got to Wendy, and again she took off at a gallop.

Suzanne was feeling great. She had been missing something, and now she knew what it was. And it was sure a lot easier than running on concrete.

She had gone a couple of miles when she saw the cattle coming up on her left and Wendy just ahead, sitting astride her horse and watching her.

Suzanne ran up to her but didn't stop, forcing Wendy to follow her in order to say, "What are you going to do if a bull catches sight of you?"

Suzanne ignored her.

"You know what a bull's going to do if he sees that red shirt of yours?"

"That's an old wives' tale, Wendy; bulls are color-blind."

Wendy took off at a gallop again and this time Suzanne had the feeling she wasn't going to stop. She had an idea that Wendy would want to get back to the ranch first and tell her side of it.

Well, let her. Suzanne was enjoying herself.

BACK AT THE RANCH, the kids were the first to see Wendy riding in. Billy's oldest nephew, Mickey, ran up to him and said, "Aunt Wendy's coming but not that other lady."

"Are you sure?"

"I'm sure, Uncle Billy."

"I'll go see what's happening," said his mother, getting up and going to the end of the porch. "It's just Wendy," she called back to them. "Suzanne will probably be right behind her."

"She better be," said Billy.

A couple of minutes later Wendy was pulling up in front of the porch, a stubborn look on her face. "Did Danny Boy show up?"

"You better explain that question," said Billy, feeling a tightening in his gut.

"Your girlfriend's all right."

"What happened?" asked Bos.

"Danny Boy threw her and then took off."

Billy started to pull himself up out of his chair, reaching for his crutches.

"What are you going to do, ride to her rescue?" asked Wendy.

"No, I'm going to wring your throat."

"She's okay, Billy. She refused to let me ride her back."

"How far away were you when it happened?"

"To the foothills."

"Hell, Wendy, that's at least ten miles."

"What was I supposed to do? She wanted to run back."

"Run ten miles?" asked Ginger.

But Billy was sitting back with a smile. He didn't have a doubt in the world that Suzanne would make it.

Mike said to Wendy, "Go after her with another horse. Otherwise your name's going to be mud around here."

"I was going to," said Wendy, "that's what I came back for."

"Well, get a move on, girl," said Bos.

"Maybe I should go after her on my dirt bike," said Ginger.

"No, Mother, I'll take her a horse," said Wendy. "Actually, she was riding pretty well up until that happened. I never thought she'd get that far." There was grudging respect in her voice that didn't escape Billy's notice.

WHEN WENDY SHOWED UP with the extra horse, Suzanne was just getting her second wind. She just wished she was wearing running shorts and a lighter shirt as her clothes were soaked through with sweat and adding weight she didn't need.

Wendy tried to block her path, but Suzanne veered around her, not even breaking stride. She had never run as well before and was wondering if there were marathons in Wyoming. If not, maybe she'd start one.

"You don't have to be so stubborn," said Wendy, riding up next to her and pacing her.

"Leave me alone, I'm enjoying myself."

"I thought you were enjoying the ride."

"I was, but this feels good."

"I think you're trying to make me look bad."

"Right, Wendy. I jumped off my horse and shooed him away just so I could run home and make you look bad." Except there was a kernel of truth in what Wendy said.

"You trying to prove something?"

"Not to you," said Suzanne. "Why don't you get off that horse and run with me?"

"You think I can't?"

"I'd be pretty surprised if you could in those boots you're wearing. I'd have a hard time just walking around the city in those."

"I would imagine you walk around the city in four-inch heels."

"Just another one of your misconceptions, Wendy. You ought to try getting out of Wyoming and see how the rest of the world lives."

To her surprise, Wendy burst out laughing. "You give my brother this hard a time?"

"Sometimes."

Wendy seemed to be thinking that over. Suzanne hoped she took her time about it because it was getting harder by the minute to talk and run at the same time.

She finally said, "You going to marry my brother?" and she sounded friendlier, in fact almost human.

"No."

"That's the way it looks to me."

"As I said before, Wendy—"

"I remember. Another of my misconceptions."

"That doesn't mean I'm ruling out other possibilities, however."

At that, Wendy mercifully took a break with her questions and rode along beside her in silence.

Suzanne finally broke the silence by saying, "I don't suppose you'd loan me that scarf you're wearing around your neck."

Wendy untied the kerchief and handed it down to her. Suzanne folded it up and tied it around her forehead to

keep the sweat out of her eyes. It was getting so bad the
landscape was becoming blurred.

"You're really sweating," said Wendy.

"No kidding."

"You've only got about another mile to go."

"And just when I was getting warmed up."

"I wish the rest of the family could hear you. They
wouldn't believe me if I told them about the mouth you
have on you."

Suzanne just smiled.

"THEY'RE COMING, THEY'RE COMING," yelled Mickey,
rounding the side of the house at a run. He tripped over
his own feet and sat down hard, grinning up at them.

Everyone got up and trooped off the porch, leaving
Billy sitting there. He debated trying the stairs on
crutches by himself and decided to stay where he was. He
wanted to get his leg fit, not hurt it again. He couldn't
wait to be the one to take Suzanne on a ride around the
ranch.

He smiled when he heard a cheer go up. God damn,
but she was some woman. She was showing his sister up
and that was something he'd never seen done before.
Wendy must be having conniption fits.

Wendy came riding around to the front of the porch
and pulled up in front of where he was seated. "Hey,
Billy?"

"Yeah?"

"She's okay."

"I know."

"No, I don't mean okay. I mean *okay*."

"I knew what you meant," said Billy, and then he saw
Suzanne rounding the house, her arms raised high above
her head as though she were crossing a finish line.

She came to a halt in front of the porch and grinned up at him.

"You know something, Suzanne? You're just like my sister—you're both show-offs."

Suzanne stuck her tongue out at him.

THEY WERE SITTING out on the porch having coffee and blueberry pie and watching the sun go down when a familiar-looking pickup pulled up behind Mike's station wagon.

Suzanne was just putting two and two together when the door on the passenger side opened and Mouse got out.

Hardly believing her eyes, Suzanne watched as Mouse tentatively approached the porch.

"Mom?" Mouse said, sounding very unsure of herself, which wasn't at all like Mouse, and the "Mom?" was immediately echoed by several people on the porch.

Next to her, Billy began to chuckle, and Suzanne didn't know what he found so amusing because personally she was worried over what Mouse was doing here when she had left her safely at college.

Before Suzanne could explain to Billy's family that yes, she was a mother, Mouse looked at Daryl, who had come up beside her, and then she looked back at Suzanne and said, "Daryl and I just got married."

And then all hell broke loose.

Chapter Twelve

Mouse felt she had lucked out.

She had expected to see just her mom and Billy; the other guests turned out to be a bonus. Mouse had seen the shock on her mother's face when she told her she and Daryl had gotten married, but with all the people around, her mom couldn't say much. She couldn't say something like, "Well, you can just get it annulled." By the time everyone left and she had to talk to her mom alone, maybe things would've cooled down. And Billy would be there. She had a feeling Billy would be on her side.

Mouse didn't see how it was possible since her mom had practically just gotten here, but Suzanne seemed right at home with Billy's family. If anyone had told Mouse when they left New York that in a few days' time her mother would be sitting on a ranch in Wyoming and looking like she belonged, Mouse would have thought they needed a shrink. Her sophisticated New York mom looking at home on some ranch? It wouldn't have seemed conceivable at the time, and yet she seemed to fit in with these people. Her mom looked quite at home sitting on a porch in Wyoming; in fact she seemed to fit into the landscape better here than she ever had in New York. It was as though she had finally found the place that best fit her.

Mouse and Daryl had been given pie and coffee and chairs had been brought out for them. Daryl wasn't saying anything, leaving it all to her, even though it had been Daryl's idea to come here. Which didn't seem fair since it had been Daryl's idea to get married. And then, as they drove here, Daryl started to chicken out. The warm welcome Daryl had initially envisioned was slowly changed to one of her mother pointing a shotgun at him and blowing him away.

Not that Mouse had objected to getting married. On the contrary, she thought it was the perfect idea. She loved the idea that she was going straight to marriage when she had never even gone steady, and she only wished her girlfriends back in New York knew about it.

Mouse figured that if she were going to attempt to get her mother to agree to let her drop out of college, arguing from the position of a married woman would give her some power. Which wasn't to say that Mouse hadn't wanted to marry Daryl. It's just that she would love him whether they were married or not and the legality of it made very little difference to her.

She thought it would make a difference to her mom, though. Mothers always wanted their daughters to get married, didn't they? Wasn't that the ultimate maternal wish? Not that Suzanne had actually ever said anything to that effect, but since her friends' mothers had often voiced that wish she was pretty sure it was universal. She hoped it was universal. If it wasn't, she was in deep trouble.

Mouse sat eating the pie and sizing up the gathering. Daryl was talking quietly with Billy's brother and sister-in-law down at the other end of the porch. They seemed to be the least surprised by Mouse's appearance and the least important to Billy as far as approval went. Well, Daryl could stay there out of the center of the action. He wouldn't be much help when it came to convincing her mother that she didn't need college, anyway.

Billy's sister—and Mouse would have recognized her anywhere—had been the first to speak when Mouse announced she was married. She had turned to Suzanne, a look of incredulity on her face, and said, "You have a daughter?" It sounded like she was asking Suzanne if she had a social disease.

She could see that Billy's parents seemed surprised at Mouse's existence, too. Mouse was surprised that her mother hadn't even told these people about her. Was she trying to keep her a secret? And, if so, why? Boy, only a couple of days out of her mother's sight and she seemed to have become forgotten.

Billy hadn't looked at all surprised by the news. Billy had looked amused. But then Billy had known all along what was going on with her and Daryl.

Billy's dad was looking at her with interest and his mom was minding her own business but staying within earshot. Neither Billy nor his sister looked one bit like either one of their parents.

There were three little boys playing hide-and-seek around all the cars and Mouse didn't have a clue who they were.

Suzanne, though, was clearly shocked. Maybe she should have hinted a little to her mom on the trip that she and Daryl were more than driving companions. Well, it was too late now; now she knew. Now she was aware that Mouse had to have sneaked around and lied to her or else she and Daryl had managed the fastest romance in the world.

Mouse kept waiting for her mom to ask her how they got married and why they got married and about a million other questions, but her mom seemed to be waiting for something. Maybe for a chance to question her alone. Mouse didn't want to be questioned alone. Mouse wanted to get it all out into the open and take her chances that at least part of the gathering would back her decision.

Her mom had only said one thing so far. When Billy's dad had said, "Well, I guess congratulations are in order," Suzanne had merely said, "We'll see."

Mouse decided that the suspense had been allowed to build up long enough. It was making her nervous. She had been nervous to begin with but it was getting worse. And anyway, even an idiot could plainly see that everyone was dying of curiosity and wasn't about to tackle another subject of conversation until this one was satisfied.

Mouse swallowed the last piece of pie. "I guess you're surprised," she said to her mom, which was maybe the biggest understatement of the year.

Suzanne managed a smile but the smile didn't hold much warmth. "I had no idea you and Daryl...." She let the words fade out as though not wanting to take the thought to its conclusion.

Mouse wished she hadn't finished her pie so quickly.

SUZANNE WAS PRETTY MUCH in a state of shock. Mouse couldn't be married. Mouse was only eighteen, just out of high school, starting college. Mouse wasn't even grown up yet. Not that a lot of eighteen-year-olds didn't get married, but Mouse had never even dated much and had never had a real boyfriend.

And how could her daughter possibly have made a decision that quickly? Had it been because for the first time in her life she had been left on her own? Had Suzanne misjudged in sending her daughter away to school? Had Mouse been so lonely without her mother around that she married the first guy she saw? And what was Daryl doing still hanging around the campus after Suzanne and Billy had left?

Suzanne looked around and saw that Billy's family was expecting her to say something. It wasn't that she didn't have a lot to say, or at least a lot of questions to ask, but she barely knew these people and now they were being included in what she felt should be a private conversation between her and Mouse. And no one looked ready to leave.

"Was it a justice of the peace?" Suzanne asked her, although the answer to that didn't interest her much. It wasn't the mechanics of the marriage that interested her; it was the reasons for it.

Mouse was nodding.

"Why didn't you wait? Didn't it occur to you that I might like to see you being married?"

"I thought you'd try to stop it."

"I can't stop you doing what you want, Mouse. I might have advised you to wait, but I couldn't have stopped you."

"Oh, I don't know," said Wendy, "you can be pretty formidable, Suzanne."

"You're calling *me* formidable?"

Wendy grinned. "Yeah. Not to mention stubborn, unreasonable and a few other things."

Under ordinary circumstances Suzanne would have been pleased to hear that as she had a feeling these were compliments coming from Wendy.

"Suzanne?" said Billy. "Why don't you two go in the house and talk. We're not giving you any privacy out here."

Mouse looked as though Billy had betrayed her, but Suzanne gave him a look of thanks. "I think that's a good idea. Let's go inside, Mouse."

"You want to talk to Daryl, too?"

"No, just you," said Suzanne.

Once in the house, Mouse walked around looking at the piano and the loom and anything else she could find to look at. Suzanne sat down on the couch and waited for Mouse to settle down enough to talk.

Her daughter finally sat down at the other end of the couch, curling her legs beneath her. "Okay, go on, start yelling at me," said Mouse.

"THAT MUST HAVE BEEN an interesting trip you took," Ginger said to Billy.

Billy chuckled. "The problem is, it was more interesting than Suzanne was aware of. I don't think she had any idea Mouse and Daryl were interested in each other."

"Did they run his car off a cliff, too?" asked Wendy.

"No. He was the cop where mine was run over." And then that precipitated more questions and pretty soon Billy was relating all the high points of the trip while Daryl filled in a few of the details Billy hadn't known about and left out what must have been a whole lot of others.

"I DON'T SEE WHAT'S THE BIG DEAL," said Mouse. "You ran off and got married in college."

"Do you have to make the same mistakes I made?"

"Well, at least Daryl isn't a rock musician."

"That was the best thing about your father," said Suzanne. "I happen to like rock musicians."

"Just because yours turned out to be a mistake doesn't mean mine will."

"Oh, Mouse, you haven't even had any experience. I had dated a lot before I met your father."

"And it didn't help, did it? Anyway, I'm in love, Mom. I really am."

"So was I. And it was mostly passion."

Mouse looked a bit uncomfortable at that and Suzanne was about to say something else, something along the lines of love being a lot more than sex, only that wasn't quite true. Sex had a lot to do with it. Suzanne could easily remember her first experience of sex and she knew it was the kind of earth-shattering experience that left one thinking that nothing else would ever be quite so wonderful again. And, in a way, that was true. There was something about firsts that made them memorable.

"Well, I'm not getting a divorce no matter what you say."

"I wasn't going to suggest you get a divorce, Mouse. I'll be sorry you'll be missing out on a normal college social life, but since you're married, I hope it works out. And I have nothing at all against Daryl. What's he going to do, try to get a job in Boulder?"

"We both are."

"You don't have to work, Mouse. I'll certainly continue to put you through school."

"The thing is, Mom—"

"Don't even say it, Mouse."

"Well, I've been telling you for a whole year but you wouldn't listen to me."

"That's because you don't know what you're talking about. Just because you didn't like high school doesn't mean you won't like college. They're totally different."

"I'll go later, like you're doing."

"Mouse. I happened to luck into a good-paying job, but if I hadn't, I would have had a very hard time supporting the two of us. I'd really like to see you prepare for a career of some kind. I'm not asking that you be a physicist, just something you could support yourself at."

"Daryl's going to support me."

"Where did I go wrong? Where did you get this notion that a man's supposed to support you?"

"It's not my notion, it's Daryl's. I'd like to get a job, though; I don't want to just stay home and watch soap operas."

"Look, Mouse, could we compromise? Would you try college just for one semester?"

"You can get eighty percent of my tuition back, I already asked."

"It's not the money."

"I don't want to go to college right now. I don't want to have to study every night. What's Daryl supposed to do, help me with my homework?"

Suzanne decided to quit arguing. Let Mouse see what it was like to be married for six months and work at the kind of job she was qualified for, which wasn't much. Maybe in six months she'd be ready to go to college. At the moment, if Suzanne forced the issue, Mouse would no doubt flunk out anyway.

"All right. What do you want for a wedding present?"

"Are you serious, Mom? I don't have to go to college?"

"Mouse, I never could've forced you."

Mouse relaxed with a smile. "Maybe a TV set. Or a stereo. Could we have both?"

"Where do you plan to live? Are you going back to Ohio?"

"We talked about that but we both like it out here. In fact it's really pretty around here."

"You're not moving in with me, Mouse."

"I wasn't planning on it," said Mouse, managing to sound extremely insulted. "I know you want your own space."

"I would think you and Daryl would, too."

"We do. It's just that until we find jobs and a place to live...."

"I'm only staying here this weekend," said Suzanne, "and then I'm driving on. I'll probably be back, I'm thinking of going to school here, and Billy and I ... well, we've gotten rather close."

"Are you saying you're deserting me?"

"I'll tell you what, Mouse. Since I'm saving eighty percent of your college tuition, I'll make you a wedding present of it. That should get you a TV, a stereo and a place to live for a few months."

"But you are coming back, aren't you?"

Suzanne nodded.

"Will you be living here?"

"No, I thought I'd get a place in Laramie. I'd like to go to school there."

"It's funny, isn't it? I'm married and you're going to go to college."

"Very funny," said Suzanne. "In fact I guess I'd say it's about the last thing I expected to come out of this trip."

His brother had left first, saying he better get the kids home before they started destroying the house. His dad left next, and then his mom, and Wendy left soon after, saying don't wait up for her.

It was just the four of them in the house and it was reminiscent of the night in the cabin. Only this time everyone knew what was going on with everyone else and it seemed to be making most of them uncomfortable.

"Don't you even have a TV?" asked Mouse, having investigated every corner of the living room.

"Afraid not," said Billy. "No puzzles, either."

"Billy plays the piano," said Suzanne.

Nobody took her up on that to Billy's relief. "I guess we could make an early night of it," he suggested, but that didn't go over very well, either. He had a feeling that Daryl wasn't eager to go to bed with his mother-in-law under the same roof, and he thought Suzanne and Mouse were looking uncomfortable over the idea, too. He was beginning to wish Wendy hadn't gone to town. At least when she was around she livened things up.

"So, you kids have any plans?" asked Billy. No one had let him in on what had gone on in the discussion Suzanne had with her daughter.

"We're thinking of settling out here," said Daryl. "I'll probably apply to the police department or sheriff's department or whatever they have."

"You talking about Wyoming or Colorado?" asked Billy.

Daryl and Mouse exchanged glances. "We think maybe Wyoming," said Mouse.

"Well, we're always glad to have new blood," said Billy, picturing all the young girls in town copying Mouse's example and suddenly sporting short skirts and punk haircuts. It ought to make a change, anyway.

"They'll be looking for a place to rent," said Suzanne. "Do you know of anything?"

"Not many to be found around here," said Billy. "People don't move around much."

"Well, we'll have to get the newspapers tomorrow and take a look," said Suzanne.

"Will we be able to stay here tonight?" Mouse asked Billy.

"Sure, you guys can take my room. Your mom can bunk down here with me." He saw the looks of consternation all around and said, "Hey, I think we all need to relax about this. You guys are married so naturally you'll be sharing a room. It's a given; it's nothing to be embarrassed about. And there's plenty of room down here for you mom. As a matter of fact she slept down here last night because Wendy's snoring was keeping her awake."

Mouse was turning a bright pink and even Daryl was avoiding everyone's eyes by finding something very interesting to stare at on the floor. Only Suzanne was looking amused.

"What can I tell you?" asked Billy, looking around at them.

Suzanne said, "If you're trying to diffuse the situation, Billy, you're not succeeding."

"Maybe we should get a hotel room somewhere," said Daryl.

"Wouldn't hear of it," said Billy. "I have a perfectly good bed upstairs that's not being used because I can't manage the steps."

"Couldn't we talk about something else?" asked Mouse, a pleading note in her voice.

"You sure get pretty sunsets here," said Daryl.

"Just one more thing," said Billy, "and then we can all talk about the weather. I just want to warn you about the acoustics in this house. If you sigh upstairs, the sound carries all the way to the kitchen.''

When this announcement was met with what could only be called a pregnant silence, Billy said, ''I think there's a couple of bottles of champagne in the kitchen somewhere left over from the big birthday celebration my sister orchestrates for us every year. You want to take a look in the cupboards, Mouse?''

And that suggestion, when implemented, was what finally saved the day. It turned out that neither Mouse nor Suzanne held their champagne very well and by the time they all finally did turn in for the night, no one even gave a damn about the acoustics because no one was able to stay awake long enough to find out if they were as good as Billy had said they were.

Chapter Thirteen

Suzanne was loading her bags into the back of the Suzuki before eight o'clock on Monday, wanting to get an early start. It wasn't in order to miss the heat of the day, because the heat wasn't bad in Wyoming. There wasn't the kind of humidity she was used to, and the nights were even developing a chill.

She wanted to get an early start before Mouse started asking her how to cook breakfast and where to look for an apartment and what kind of job she should look for. Those kinds of questions were Daryl's responsibility to answer now, and, of course, Mouse's. The sooner Mouse learned to make her own decisions the better off she'd be. Maybe she should have given Mouse more responsibility as she grew up, but it was always so much easier just to do the things or make the decisions herself.

And thank heavens she didn't have to spend another night under the same roof as her daughter and son-in-law. Every time she turned over on the couch she was sure Mouse would think something was going on downstairs, and every time she heard noise from up above, she was sure something was going on up there, even though nothing likely was with Wendy in the next room.

She had said goodbye to everyone the night before, with a special goodbye to Billy, so after locking up the back of the car, she got into the driver's seat and was warming up the motor when Billy came out of the house.

He came over to her open window and said, "Could you give me a hand with my bag?"

Suzanne felt something tug at her heart. "I promised you I wasn't disappearing, Billy. I'll only be gone a week."

"Not without me you won't."

"Don't think I wouldn't like you along; it's just that I think you should start physical therapy."

"It'll wait a week. You can help me with my exercises."

Suzanne only hesitated a moment, then opened the door and went back into the house. There was a leather satchel sitting by the door and she picked it up and hurried back outside. Billy was already seated in the passenger seat looking smugly satisfied. Well, she felt satisfied, too. It hadn't been easy getting up and preparing to leave without Billy. She would have missed him like crazy.

Suzanne pulled away from the house with as much speed as the Suzuki could handle. The exhilarating sense of freedom she had experienced at times on the trip was coming back to her. She could go wherever she wanted and no one could stop her. Of course Billy could try, but he wouldn't succeed.

"You act like you're making a getaway," said Billy.

"I feel like I am."

"Well, I'm glad I'm with you or I'd have gotten the idea you were in a hurry to get away from me."

"No, not you. I think I'm escaping from being a mother-in-law."

"You're doing fine at it."

"I don't know what I'm doing. I'm finding it difficult to go from thinking of Mouse as a child to Mouse as a married woman."

"It's an adjustment, I guess. I think Mouse is still trying to adjust to it, too."

Billy threw his hat in the back seat and stuck his arm out the window, giving a little cowboy yell as he did it. "Is this great being on the road again, or what?"

"It feels more normal," said Suzanne. "This car's beginning to seem like home."

"Maybe we should just drive around for the rest of our lives. If we keep changing the scenery, maybe we'll never get tired of each other."

"Is that what you're afraid of, Billy?"

"No, but I think you are."

Suzanne looked at him in surprise. "What gives you that idea?"

"You were off looking for adventure, weren't you?"

"Don't you think it's pretty adventurous for a New York woman to be driving around the wild west with a cowboy?"

"Thank God for movies," said Billy with a grin.

"And soap operas," said Suzanne. "Whenever I think you're getting bored with me, I can switch over to Barbara Jean for a while."

Billy let out a groan.

BILLY HAD BEEN AFRAID of more than getting tired of each other. He had woken up that morning and seen Suzanne packing and had pretended to be still asleep. And it was fear that made him pretend; fear that she was driving off and never coming back, despite her promise not to disappear.

Sure, her daughter was there, and sure she'd come back and see her, but there was nothing stopping her from viewing Montana in an even more favorable light than Wyoming or even meeting up with a faster-talking cowboy who would steal her away.

That wasn't going to happen if he could help it. He'd be damned if she was going to get away from him now that he'd found her.

So when she said, "There's a stop I want to make in Laramie before we leave. I want to see if I can possibly get into the university this fall," he had felt a great deal of relief. At least her intention had been to come back. And he didn't think it was just because of the school, either, because there were schools in every state.

"They'll let you in," he assured her.

"Without teaching? I appreciated your father's suggestion, but I feel foolish enough being recognized as Barbara Jean without promoting that image in the communications department. Anyway, communications doesn't interest me."

"What does interest you?"

Suzanne flashed him a smile. "You mean besides you?"

"You felt I needed a little reassurance?"

"I thought you might."

"Well, I guess I did, and I thank you."

"Something totally different from anything I've ever done. Maybe something involving math or science. I have this theory—only recently developed—that it's a good thing to totally change the course of your life at least once. I mean, what if every doctor decided one day to spend the next twenty years being a cowboy? I bet it would make a lot of them happy.''

"Maybe make a lot of patients unhappy,'' said Billy.

"Maybe not.''

"Am I getting a hint here?''

"No hint; I'm serious. I never again want to do anything connected to communications or entertainment. It might have been lucrative, but it was never satisfying.''

"Why were you an actress if it didn't interest you?''

"I was never an actress, Billy.''

"Let me get this straight. You spent years on *Reach for the Sky*, but you weren't an actress?''

"That's right.''

"I'm a little confused.''

"I was a secretary at ABC, working to support me and Mouse, and one day I was asked if I wanted to read for the part of someone new being written into the soap. I think they thought I was an actress. Just about all the secretaries there were.''

"And I guess you got the part.''

Suzanne nodded. "It didn't require much acting. I just had to read the cue cards and act sweet and a little dumb.''

"So if you hated it so much, why didn't you do something else?''

"Because the only thing I knew how to do was type. I hadn't prepared for any kind of work. Anyway, it paid well, and I wanted Mouse to have the kind of life I had had growing up. I didn't want to bring her up in some cold-water flat with rats.''

"Now you're beginning to sound like a soap opera.''

"That's all I could afford in New York until I got on the soap. We didn't have rats, though; that was an exaggeration. But we had roaches almost that big."

"So I guess it was worth it."

"Sure it was. I was able to send Mouse to private schools, buy my apartment and invest in real estate. If I'm careful, I could afford to go to school the rest of my life."

Billy turned to look at her. "Is that what you're planning on doing?"

"Do you have any objection?"

He shrugged. "I guess it would keep you out of trouble. What you said before, about thinking everyone should change the course of their life at least once, were you trying to say you think I ought to give up the ranch?"

"I wasn't talking about you, Billy. You seem happy and content in what you're doing. You're living the kind of idealized life most people only dream about."

"Yeah, well, the ranch is pretty and all, but I wouldn't call living with your sister when you're thirty-six ideal. And you haven't seen the place when we're buried in snow, either."

"Don't get the idea I'm moving in there with you, Billy."

"I didn't think you would."

"It's not just the fact that it's not big enough for all three of us, or that I'd feel like a third cog."

"We have plenty of property to build another house on." In fact he already had the spot picked out in his mind, a place with maybe the most perfect view in all the world. And this time he'd make sure the acoustics were right.

When they got to the university, Suzanne left him in the car while she went into the administration building. A half hour later she came out smiling.

"They were glad to get you, right?" asked Billy.

"They made it so easy. They'll send for my transcripts, but they said there'd be no problem with my starting this fall. And I have two weeks before school starts."

"You'll have to talk Mouse out of all those college clothes you bought her."

"You're talking about her most prized possessions. Anyhow, those are going to be the last clothes Mouse gets from Bloomingdale's for a good long time, I imagine. She better treasure them."

"So where are we off to? Not that it matters."

"I thought Wyoming, Idaho and then up into Washington if we have the time. What do you think?"

"Sounds good to me. Hell, it's almost like we're going on the honeymoon the kids are missing out on."

"At that age, every day's going to seem like a honeymoon to them."

"Hell, it's beginning to seem that way at my age," said Billy.

"A GARAGE APARTMENT?" said Mouse.

The real-estate woman nodded. "That's about it. It's quite nice, though. Now if you were a student the university would find you housing."

"No way," said Mouse, who had seen Daryl's look. "I'd rather live in a garage apartment than go to school."

"It's only a hundred and twenty-five a month," said the realtor.

Mouse cheered up. That kind of money wouldn't even pay the phone bill in New York, at least according to her mother, who had always complained about the phone bill. "Okay, let's go see it."

It turned out to be surrounded by trees on three sides, which made Mouse feel like she was in a tree house when she looked out the windows. It had three rooms and was partially furnished and it looked a lot better to her than her room at home or the dorm at college. And with Daryl there with her it ought to be perfect. It had all the appliances and a bed and a table and chairs and some living-room furniture. They'd need a TV first thing, and maybe some sheets for the bed. And if not a stereo, at least a cassette player so she could listen to her tapes.

"What do you think?" asked the realtor.

"I think it's great," said Mouse.

"Is it on a lease or month-to-month?" asked Daryl, who sounded as though he knew what he was talking about. Mouse was glad of that as she didn't know the first thing about renting an apartment.

"I think they'll rent either way."

"Could we move in today?" asked Mouse.

"I don't see why not," said the woman.

"Maybe we ought to think about it," said Daryl.

"What's to think about?" said Mouse. "It's the only thing available, we like it, and it's reasonable. And all we'll really need is a TV."

"You'll need to provide your own kitchen things and linens," said the realtor.

But Mouse was way ahead of her. Having never learned to cook, Mouse figured they could eat their meals out.

SUZANNE WAS CHARMED by Buffalo, Wyoming, and even more charmed by the bed-and-breakfast inn they found to stay at. There was an enormous old four-poster bed with a feather mattress that was not particularly good for Billy's leg, but he didn't seem to be complaining.

"With the way we're sunk down, this might be an impossibility," said Billy, grinning up at her.

"I'm not ready to give up," said Suzanne, wondering if they could move the mattress onto the floor.

"Just think," said Billy. "Right at this very moment your daughter and Daryl could be making you a grandchild."

"Oh, my God, why did you say that?"

"I couldn't help it. It just came into my mind."

"Billy, I've never even talked to her about birth control."

"I think kids learn all that at school. And if not from school, from their friends."

"But she's not *on* any."

"I wouldn't worry about it."

Suzanne carefully moved off Billy and sat on the edge of the bed. "I think I ought to call her."

"Suzanne, you're overreacting. I was just kidding you. Anyway, I'm sure Daryl knows all about birth control."

"I thought Mouse's father did, too."

"You want to go back, Suzanne? Although if they don't know anything about it, it's probably too late anyway."

"I don't want to go back. I want to call her."

Billy pushed himself up and put a couple of pillows behind him. "You'll have to call from downstairs."

"I know. Do you mind?"

"Go on. See if you can get us something hot to drink while you're down there."

THE DOOR WAS SLOWLY pushed open and Suzanne came in carrying two mugs of tea. "Well?" he asked her.

"Wendy says they moved into an apartment in Laramie."

"Already?"

Suzanne handed him a mug and sat in the chair next to the bed. "She says it's over a garage."

"It sounds like something they can afford."

"I never thought my daughter would be living over a garage."

"It's probably not bad at all. Laramie doesn't exactly have slum dwellings. Anyway, think back. I bet you wouldn't have minded living over a garage with Sweet Basil."

"You remember his name?"

"I remember everything you've told me."

"No, I wouldn't have minded. I wouldn't mind now. It's just that I've rather spoiled Mouse."

"Well, look at it this way. If they were smart enough to find an apartment already, then they're probably smart enough to use birth control."

"That's what Wendy said."

"You told my sister about this?"

"She said she'd have a talk with Mouse."

"God, I'd love to hear that," said Billy. "Now come back to bed. And, incidentally, what are *you* doing about birth control?"

"The great cowboy hero finally asks," said Suzanne, grabbing one of the pillows and hitting him with it.

"I figured you knew what you were doing," said Billy, then dodged the second pillow.

"I do, and that doesn't include getting pregnant. Do you mind?"

"Me? Why should I mind? If we feel the need to play with babies, we'll play with Mouse's."

"Don't say that! Now you've got me worried again."

THEY WERE ONLY MILES from Montana when Suzanne said, "Let's go back."

"Are you still worried about Mouse? You know it's too late to worry about that."

"I want to find a place to live, get settled."

"I knew it: you're tired of me already."

Suzanne pulled into a rest area and made a U-turn. "I'm not tired of you, Billy. I think I'm finally getting tired of driving."

"You're worried about Mouse."

"I'm not worried about Mouse. I worry more about you than I worry about Mouse. And I think you ought to go to a doctor for a checkup and start your physical therapy. You're going to be sorry if you let it wait too long and you're never able to get on a horse again."

"I know you picture me riding out on the range."

"Don't you?"

"Sure. Sometimes. But most of the time I drive my Ford Bronco."

"I want to find a place to live in Laramie and fix it up and get my schoolbooks...."

"It's hard to find rentals in Laramie."

"Then I'll buy a place. I wouldn't mind one of those Victorian-looking houses with a front porch and a big yard."

"Do I get to visit?"

"I was thinking, Billy. Since your physical therapy will be in Laramie, why don't you stay with me and commute to the ranch when you need to be there?"

"Hell, Suzanne, ranchers don't commute."

"Why not?"

"I don't know why not. They just don't, that's all."

"Fine. Then you can live at home and we'll date. Only on weekends, though; I'll have to study on school nights."

"Out-and-out blackmail," said Billy.

Suzanne shot the Suzuki out onto the highway and headed in the direction of Laramie.

"If you loved me, you wouldn't make me commute."

"If I didn't love you, you'd be back on the ranch right now."

"That a fact?"

Suzanne nodded.

"Can't you just say it?"

"I already did."

"That was a sneaky, roundabout way."

Suzanne looked over at him and grinned. "I love you madly, Billy Blue."

"That's better. Well, with that settled, then I have to say that the idea of commuting doesn't sound all that bad. It's not as though it's any great distance."

"That's true."

"And since you're one of those rich soap-opera stars, you'll probably keep me in luxurious surroundings."

"Absolutely. We can even get a hot tub."

"Doggone if I wasn't lucky your kid knocked my car over that cliff."

"Actually we planned that."

"You *what*?"

"Well, I've always had this thing for cowboys, and when we pulled into that lookout point, Mouse said, 'Hey, Mom, there's the man of your dreams.' And I looked over and saw you standing there, a cowboy on crutches in the middle of Ohio, and I said, 'Mouse, hit his car over the cliff, I've got to have that man.' The rest is history."

There was a long silence from Billy. Then, "Damned if I don't think it's possible."

"And it worked out perfectly. I got you, didn't I?"

"You made that up, didn't you?"

"Did I?"

"I'm trying to remember how long it took you to pull in there and then hit my car."

"Mouse was driving very slowly."

"What if someone had been in the car?"

"You've got to take some risks in life, Billy."

"I guess you'd call that love at first sight."

Suzanne suppressed a smile.

"You're having me on, aren't you? This is just one of those New York actressy tricks of yours. It's probably word for word one of Barbara Jean's lines."

"Give me credit for a little more creativity than that, Billy."

"You really got me wondering now, Suzanne. Here I thought I was deviously pursuing you, and now you say that all the time it was the other way around."

"Does that bother you?"

"Not a hell of a lot."

"Good."

"But I still think you're lying."

Suzanne chuckled. "But you'll never really know for sure, will you, Billy?"

Epilogue

There were two feet of snow outside the freshly painted white Victorian house with blue shutters, and more coming down. Suzanne, who used to wish for a white Christmas in New York, had already had a white Thanksgiving and they'd even had a few flurries on Halloween.

Mouse and Daryl had stopped by earlier with their kitten for her to baby-sit while they took off skiing for the weekend. They had looked happy and still madly in love and Suzanne had real hopes for their marriage. Mouse had already progressed from a somewhat spoiled girl to a working woman who stuck to her budget and was talking about night classes at college next semester, and Daryl had gotten on with the sheriff's department and was learning to be a gourmet cook. Mouse and Suzanne's relationship was gradually changing from mother and daughter to friends, and Suzanne, who missed her women friends, was finding that satisfying.

She still kept up with her New York friends, but now they seemed to be scattering: Marielle to Chicago, Jaime to New Orleans and Abbie out to California. The building wouldn't seem the same if she did return, although she would one day in order to sell her apartment. Also, back in the city, *Reach for the Sky* had finally given up on her, and Barbara Jean had been killed off for good.

Suzanne turned on the lamps and admired the way the living room looked with the white furniture and blue calico curtains and slipcovers. Billy had said, "Blue and white? You're doing the entire house in blue and white?" but when she had pointed out that the shade of blue exactly matched his eyes, he had looked secretly pleased. And she loved it, particularly after having lived fifteen years with hi-tech furnishings. They had seemed the height of sophistication to her when she'd bought them, but they had never seemed warm and comfortable.

"Suzanne?" she heard Billy calling. "Come here a minute, I want to show you something."

She picked up the kitten and carried him to the two rooms she had converted into one for an exercise room. There was a treadmill for her for when the snow was too deep to run and several machines the physical therapist had suggested she get for Billy. With her encouragement and his determination he was now off a cane and building up his muscles.

He was on the exercycle, sweat pouring off him. "Watch this," he said, his eyes on the computerized printout. "I'm going to do a mile today and my leg is hardly even sore."

Suzanne stood beside him and when he reached the mile mark, she cheered. "By spring you ought to be running with me."

"Don't get your hopes up about that."

"I'll be your personal trainer."

"To tell you the truth, Suzanne, running doesn't sound like much fun."

Suzanne put her arm around his shoulders and the kitten climbed from her chest over to Billy's, its little claws digging in and making Billy yelp.

"Don't tell me we're baby-sitting again."

"You know you love that kitten in our bed."

Suzanne left the kitten on Billy's chest and went over to her treadmill. She got on, turned on the switch and was starting to run when Billy said, "You going to run ten miles on that thing?"

"Did you have something better in mind?"

"I was thinking we could get in that hot tub together."

"Is that what you were thinking?" asked Suzanne, turning up the speed a little.

"My physical therapist says it's good for my sore muscles."

"Right. But he doesn't know you use your muscles when you're in there."

"I don't tell him everything," said Billy.

Suzanne stepped to the edge of the machine and turned it off. "Billy Blue, how is it I love you so much I'm willing to forgo my running to get into a hot tub with you?"

"Just pure luck, I guess."

"Oh, not entirely," she said. "I always did have a thing for cowboys."

ABOUT THE AUTHOR

Beverly Sommers's trademark is humor. And no one writes it quite like she does. Her offbeat, hilarious stories have made her one of the most popular American Romance authors. One of the original authors of the series, Beverly has been contributing since 1983 and has written fourteen American Romances.

A lover of travel, Beverly was born in Illinois, lived for a time in California and now divides her time between a New York apartment and a Miami houseboat.

Books by Beverley Sommers

HARLEQUIN AMERICAN ROMANCE

125—CHANGING PLACES
137—CONVICTIONS
152—SNOWBIRD
165—LE CLUB
179—SILENT NIGHT
191—PHOEBE'S DEPUTY
216—OF CATS AND KINGS
242—TEACHER'S PET

HARLEQUIN INTRIGUE

3—MISTAKEN IDENTITY
87—HOLD BACK THE NIGHT

ATTRACTIVE, SPACE SAVING BOOK RACK

Display your most prized novels on this handsome and sturdy book rack. The hand-rubbed walnut finish will blend into your library decor with quiet elegance, providing a practical organizer for your favorite hard-or soft-covered books.

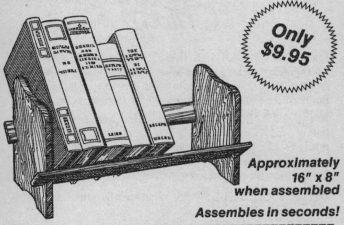

Only $9.95

Approximately 16" x 8" when assembled

Assembles in seconds!

To order, rush your name, address and zip code, along with a check or money order for $10.70* ($9.95 plus 75¢ postage and handling) payable to *Harlequin Reader Service*:

BKR-1A

Lynda Ward's TOUCH THE STARS

...the final book in the The Welles Family Trilogy

Lynda Ward's TOUCH THE STARS...the final book in the Welles Family Trilogy. All her life Kate Welles Brock has sought to win the approval of her wealthy and powerful father, even going as far as to marry Burton Welles's handpicked successor to the Corminco Corporation.

Now, with her marriage in tatters behind her, Kate is getting the first taste of what it feels like to really live. Her glorious romance with the elusive Paul Florian is opening up a whole new world to her.... Kate is as determined to win the love of her man as she is to prove to her father that she is the logical choice to succeed him as head of Corminco....

Don't miss TOUCH THE STARS, a Harlequin Superromance coming to you in September.

If you missed the first two books of this exciting trilogy, #317 RACE THE SUN and #321 LEAP THE MOON, and would like to order them, send your name, address and zip or postal code, along with a check or money order for $2.95 for each book ordered (plus $1.00 postage and handling) payable to Harlequin Reader Service to:

In the U.S.

901 Fuhrmann Blvd.
Box 1396
Buffalo, NY 14240-9954

In Canada

P.O. Box 609
Ft. Erie, Ontario
L2A 5X3

LYNDA-1C

Harlequin American Romance

COMING NEXT MONTH

#261 THE TROUBLE WITH THORNY by Lori Copeland

Chelsey Stevens was in a tizzie. As the director of Rosehaven, it was her job to keep the retirement home running smoothly, but Thorny Bradford, a new resident, had the place astir. And Thorny's son Greg wasn't any help, either. He merely overwhelmed her with his charm.

#262 NATURAL TOUCH by Cathy Gillen Thacker

As a pediatrician, Sarah thought she knew all about children. But when her best friend died and left Sarah guardian of three kids, she found out how wrong she was. Attorney David Buchanon thought Sarah to be a loving, giving woman, but did she have what it took to turn a household into a family?

#263 LOST AND FOUND by Dallas Schulze

When Sam rescued Babs Malone from kidnappers, he intended only to collect the reward and part company with the heiress. But kidnapping was only the tip of a nasty iceberg threatening Babs, and for the first time Sam found a reason for heroism— but no guarantee it would keep them alive.

#264 FIREDANCE by Vella Munn

Smoke jumper Lory Foster battled forest fires that ravaged the Northwest forests. Mike Steen battled those blazes from his specially equipped chopper. Together, they gambled everything on one glorious weekend on the drifting currents of Idaho's Snake River.

HARLEQUIN SIGNATURE EDITION

VIOLET WINSPEAR

HOUSE OF STORMS

Editorial secretary Debra Hartway travels to the Salvador family's rugged Cornish island home to work on Jack Salvador's latest book. Disturbing questions hang in the troubled air over Lovelis Island. What or who had caused the tragic death of Jack's young wife? Why did Jack stay away from the home and, more especially, the baby son he loved so well? And—why should Rodare, Jack's brother, who had proved himself a man of the highest integrity, constantly invade Debra's thoughts with such passionate, dark desires...?

Violet Winspear, who has written more than 65 romance novels translated worldwide into 18 languages, is one of Harlequin's best-loved and bestselling authors. HOUSE OF STORMS, her second title in the Harlequin Signature Edition program, is a full-length novel rich in romantic tradition and intriguingly spiced with an atmosphere of danger and mystery.

Watch for HOUSE OF STORMS—coming in October!

HOFS-1